THE
PROGRESSIVE
CHILDREN'S MINISTRY
LEADER

THE PROGRESSIVE CHILDREN'S MINISTRY LEADER

ESTHER MORENO

To order additional copies of this book, contact:
Xlibris
844-714-8691
www.Xlibris.com
Orders@Xlibris.com
825405

I dedicate this book to my dear friend Ricardo Miller who through perseverance and determination impacted a nation for Christ. Your tenacity and vision have motivated an army of Children's Ministry leaders, of which I am one.

CONTENTS

ACKNOWLEDGEMENTS

The incredible doors that God has opened for me from the inception of my ministry to reach children and families has given me pause time and time again. As I reflect on the goodness of God, those reflections are always coupled with the help and support of so many who have rallied around me and my vision since day one. Together I believe we will reach tomorrow's generation as we move beyond the status quo and make the necessary investments to become the church this generation so desperately needs. To all those who invited me on their platforms, who so graciously joined me on mine, and who entrusted their Children's Ministry teams and districts to my leadership, Thank you!

Thank you to my brilliant husband Guylando Moreno who has labored alongside me in my quest to reach the next generation. In spite of your busy schedule, I continue to be in awe of how you juggle so many plates without complaint in an effort to support me in every way. I would be remiss if I didn't thank my dear friend Sherry Chester, who spent countless hours poring over this manuscript so it could reach its utmost potential. I hope you see your thumbprint in these pages and rest in the knowledge that your contributions are enriching leaders around the world.

FOREWORD

The first time I met Esther Moreno I remember thinking, "*her cup runneth over.*" Esther clearly loves what she does. She loves children. She loves leaders. She loves empowering leaders to serve children. Leading in children's ministry is not for the faint of heart. It typically doesn't pay well. There is little to no recognition and an endless amount of work to be done. There's a reason the average ministry leader's tenure is less than three years. Ministry is messy. Children's ministry is messy with a side of glitter. It's also filled with purposeful encounters and meaningful moments that will live forever in your heart and mind *if* you are willing to stick with it, but staying power requires constant growth and reinforced fortitude. The Progressive Children's Ministry Leader is an encouraging and valuable tool for new children's ministry leaders and a refreshing review for children's ministry veterans. With practical tips, key insights and discussion questions throughout the text, it encourages problem-solving conversations and immediate application. Every leader would benefit from reading this book.

With more than 20 years in family ministry I've seen both ends of the spectrum. I've watched well qualified people crash and burn and inexperienced but passionate leaders excel and guide teams of volunteers to incredible impact. Why do some experience burnout while others find their stride? Humility. We are not enough. We will never be enough, but when we couple a willingness to learn with the counsel of our Heavenly Father we will see His kingdom advance.

The Progressive Children's Ministry Leader is clear cut guidance on how to do both. Esther's writing is heartfelt and challenging and I believe you will be blessed by her words of wisdom.

Jessica Bealer
Director of Family Ministry
Services at Generis

Progressive:

1: The act of moving forward and onward. 2: Something with fresh ideas and thinking. 3: Innovator, Advanced, Developed, Improved, Refined

INTRODUCTION

We must not settle for subpar leadership. Our ministries to children should always be advancing, improving, developing, strengthening, maturing, and progressing. In view of pandemics, societal unrest, digital threats, and widespread apathy, effective Children's Ministry leaders are needed like never before. Yet despite challenges of this present age, far too few Children's Ministry leaders are equipping themselves or their teams to effectively manage the challenges they will inevitably face.

The demands on Children's Ministry leaders in a digital age have never been greater. With the pressures of weekly programming, parents, pastors, and volunteers, Children's Ministry can be exhausting. The tyranny of the to-do list seems overwhelming. But leaders must rise to the occasion. No longer can our ministries subsist on only a love of children or natural abilities. It is not enough to operate as the church's babysitting club with scant vision or strategy. The days of doing ministry all alone or in a last-minute, frenzied, or disorganized manner must come to an end. Teams that are plagued by strife, conflict, and offense must no longer be tolerated.

Those who venture to read on should aspire to more. This resource is a clarion call to Children's Ministry leaders who recognize that they, their ministries, and their teams are worthy of investment. They deeply desire to improve how they lead. They are hungry to be more effective for the sake of the children and families they are called to serve. They know it is time for **progress.** This book is for those who are ready for next level leadership. Admittedly, the lessons, scriptures, and recommendations contained in the forthcoming pages are not for the faint of heart. You will be challenged to be deliberate and intentional about investing in your own personal growth and development. Your vision and goals for your Children's Ministry department will be tested, tried, and measured against God's standards. You will be invited to soberly examine whether your leadership optimizes or undermines teamwork. Your organizational prowess, efficiency, and ability to focus will be buffeted by best practices. Above all, the lens by which you view leadership will be sharpened by a deeper sensitivity to God's will and undergirded by a supernatural maturity that is able to overlook offense and truly value people.

If you are brave enough to start the journey toward a healthier and more effective Children's Ministry leadership, there are a few items that will enhance your experience. First, be prayerful and thoughtful about each chapter. So many leaders are great about acquiring books, but fewer are as eager to apply their knowledge. Please don't waste this opportunity. Second, lean in and deeply ponder the implications of these truths. Each chapter ends with questions to consider, individually or collectively, to spark further exploration of each truth. Beyond this, every chapter is infused with Tech Bites, technological tips that will help you work and lead more effectively in a digital age. Ready or not, it's time to become a Progressive Children's Ministry leader.

CHAPTER 1

"Think before you speak. Read before you think"
-Fran Lebowitz

PROGRESSIVE LEADERS ARE READERS

For almost two decades, I have had the privilege of serving as a Children's Ministry leader. It gives me pause every time I reflect on the incredible journey that God has taken me on through the beautiful world of Children's Ministry. It has been a journey filled with both unimaginable triumphs and a healthy share of tears. My career has brought me before more Sunday schools, children's churches, and VBS programs than I can remember, affording me the privilege to connect with kids not only in the United States but overseas as well. As a speaker and influencer, I've helped countless churches to navigate their way to a healthier and more effective Children's Ministry. But it's hard to imagine that a little Black girl from the Southside of Chicago would grow up to become a nationally-recognized Children's Ministry leader. I can still vividly remember sitting in those old, uncomfortable pews listening to my father preach behind that massive wooden podium in the pulpit. Most people don't know that I am a part of the infamous "PK" club, otherwise known as the "Preacher's Kid." Growing up in the church was a school all by itself, and as every PK can attest, I've seen it all: the good, the bad, and the ugly.

From PK to seminary, full-time ministry to Children's Ministry thought leader, my journey had exposed me to all manner of Children's Ministries, thriving and struggling. Through these experiences, I have witnessed and come to appreciate a common thread shared by the most effective ministries: **progressive leaders are readers**. I am a firm believer that if you're going to lead a department well, you must have a strong commitment to learning. You must be committed to discovering what is required to build your department to the level God has predestined it to be for the church, community, and the world.

A department that does not have a leader who values reading will be a department that finds itself struggling in many areas. Unfortunately, a lack of reading doesn't just affect the leader, but it also affects the children, families, departments, and people who have committed themselves to serve under that particular leader. How do I know this? Because that was me! Now don't get me wrong. I liked the *idea* of reading books; I just didn't read books. Like a good Children's Ministry leader, I would go to the conferences and purchase what I considered the hottest books. I even decorated my office with them, but if you wanted me to get past chapter one, you were asking for too much. Besides, I was busy doing ministry! Who had time to read a book when you're busy planning large events, general programming, and coordinating everything else? In those days I was probably busier running myself and the ministry into the ground due to my lack of knowledge. The book of Hosea reminds us of the severe consequence of operating without knowledge.

> *"My people are destroyed by a lack of knowledge"*
> *-Hosea 4:6 NIV.*

When we refuse to invest time to acquire the necessary skills, knowledge, and best practices to enhance our ministries, we destroy ourselves. We destroy our potential to be all that God has called us to be. We destroy our departments because we forfeit opportunities to reach children and families better. We destroy our credibility with those who depend upon us for next-level leadership in an ever-changing world. At the end of the day, every leader can and should discipline themselves to become a reader. True leaders are readers. **If you consider yourself a true leader to the next generation, you must commit to learning how to be engaged in not only gathering good content but reading it as well. It's through reading, and applying what you have read, that will help you become a progressive leader worthy of following.**

Benefits of Reading

Reading helps to keep us mentally sharp. Just like we exercise to keep our bodies in shape, we must do the same for our brains. There's no question that reading comes with a host of benefits from preventing cognitive decline, reducing stress, and fighting depression. According to the Harvard Business Review, the leadership benefits of reading are vast. Evidence indicates that reading can enhance intelligence by increasing verbal and emotional intelligence and lead to innovation and insight. All qualities that aid in improving one's leadership and management ability.

In particular, Anne Cunningham's research explored the reciprocal effects of reading by examining the role reading volume plays in shaping the mind. One study conducted found that reading more significantly impacted vocabulary skills, general knowledge, spelling, and verbal fluency; thus, making one a more effective communicator. After being tested on general knowledge in a later study, reading was associated with higher scores, while television exposure was associated with lower scores. This is not good news for a society that is over-reliant on television for information about the world. The whole point is that reading makes you smarter and will help you develop the qualities needed to lead well. As reading is declining, those who actively engage themselves in reading set themselves up for success.

Excuses, Excuses, Excuses

Leaders who fail to prioritize reading, personal growth, and continuous improvement will inevitably become frustrated and increasingly ineffective in their leadership. Unfortunately, their focus shifts to every other external cause for failure. Instead, they should be soberly wrestling with how their leadership (or lack thereof) may have contributed to the failure. If left unchecked, this lack of understanding and self-examination will allow your ministry to drown in a sea of excuses. These excuses cause us to point the finger at everyone else instead of owning up to our own deficiencies. Excuses like, *"No one wants to help in the Children's Ministry…,"* because you lack the knowledge of successfully recruiting and retaining volunteers. Excuses like, *"Parents just don't care…"* because you lack the knowledge of effectively partnering with parents. Excuses like, *"Senior Leadership has no care or concern for the kid's ministry…"* because you lack the knowledge on becoming a respected leader who gets invited to the table.

I know those excuses well because I've made them all before. If you've been guilty of similar excuses, know that we've all been there, and everyone has to start somewhere. Show me the perfect leader, and I'll show you a fraud because no one has it all together. In fact, I believe the most outstanding leaders aren't flawless, but those who have learned *through* their failures. So, throw every excuse out the door and choose to grow in your knowledge every day through reading.

"It's not my fault..."
should never be a phrase
said by anyone in Children's
Ministry leadership."

Remind yourself daily that everything is changing. Nothing stays the same! The need to continually educate yourself is at an all-time high. This is, in essence, why we must read. In my first book, *Children's Ministry Moving Forward*, I reminded leaders that they needed to be progressive, forward thinkers, and planners. They need to be strategic and understand people. All of these are staple attributes of an excellent leader that can be developed over time when one embraces the discipline of reading. Why? Because **reading allows you to learn from others who have already studied, achieved, or otherwise excelled in areas of ministry where you may be struggling.** If you're struggling with recruiting volunteers, there's a book on recruiting volunteers. If you're struggling with managing your department, there's a book on managing your department. If you're struggling to connect with kids, there's a book created to improve your connection with kids. **The options are endless, and the information is vast, but it's up to you to grab hold of it and utilize it in a way that enhances your leadership.**

Rejecting a commitment to invest in personal growth and development may tempt us to question our very calling and purpose. When we're failing in an area, it is easy to ask whether we belong in that area at all. **One of the greatest tragedies in Children's Ministry is when someone who has been called by God to reach the next generation for Christ completely walks away because of their lack of commitment to grow through reading.** They attempt to build a healthy department by *guessing* what they *think* might work instead of doing the necessary research to discover practical solutions. If excuses and scapegoating aren't a viable solution, they eventually succumb to the frustration when their self-reliant attempts prove ineffective. They question the very calling that God has given them because they won't pick up a book! If there is one thing I have learned in Children's Ministry, it is this. There are no shortcuts to discovering the truth. Learning and capturing truth that has the power to change our very lives requires a journey we all must take if we truly want to lead effectively.

Reading is not Enough

The truth is, if you're failing in Children's Ministry, it can probably be traced back to either: (1) you're not reading at all, or (2) you're not applying what you've read. **In reading the right books, you also need to use the truth that you've discovered. Application is king when it comes to reading.** We see this truth expressed in the parable of the wise and foolish builders:

> *Therefore anyone who hears these words of mine and puts them into practice is like a wise man who built his house on the rock. The rain came down, the streams rose, and the winds blew and beat against that house; yet it did not fall, because it had its foundation on the rock. But everyone who hears these words of mine and does not put them into practice is like a foolish man who built his house on sand. The rain came down, the streams rose, and the winds blew and beat against that house, and it fell with a great crash.*
>
> *-Matthew 7:24-27 NIV*

So, let me ask you a question. When it comes to Children's Ministry, which builder are you? If you're reading without applying, then you're building your Children's Ministry on the sand and leaving it vulnerable to the dangerous winds that can make your department fall with a mighty crash. Choose to be a leader who sets your department up for success by building it on a solid foundation by applying the truths you have learned. If you are reading this book, I know that ultimately your goal is to be the best leader possible. If you're called to serve, then you should serve well, and reading plus application is the secret sauce that will get you there. Reading will help you thrive in every area of ministry.

So, how are you struggling? Be honest. What are those loose bolts in your leadership that could use a little tightening? Regardless of what you're struggling with, I can promise you one thing. There's a book for it! If you're struggling today, make a list of some must-read books written to strengthen those weak areas. I want to provide you with ten books that I believe every Children's Ministry Leader should read. If you have read these, please go to my website or visit me on social media and share with me some of the insights you received. I would love to know some of the books that have helped you transform the way you do ministry. Let me know what books have become a must-read for you.

- *The Fabulous Reinvention of Sunday School-* by Aaron Reynolds
- *If Disney Ran Your Children's Ministry-* by Dale Hudson
- *Don't Quit-* by Jessica Bealer & Gina McClain
- *Children's Ministry Wake Up Call-* by Esther Moreno
- *Volunteers that Stick-* by Jim Wideman
- *9 Things They Didn't Teach Me in College About Children's Ministry-* by Ryan Frank
- *Resilient-* by Valerie Bell
- *Guiding Children to Discover the Bible, Navigate Technology & Follow Jesus-* by Barna Group
- *Making Your Children's Ministry The Best Hour of Every Kid's Week-* by Sue Miller & David Staal
- *It's Personal* by Reggie Joyner

"A growing church needs a growing Children's Ministry leader."

Not Just One Way

So, I have a confession to make. I am an audiobook junkie! As a busy mom, wife, speaker, trainer, and everything else in between, I struggled with finding the time to stop, read, and complete a book. Thank God, due to technological advancements, reading now comes in several forms. Audiobooks stripped me of all my excuses. These audio adventures became my gateway to an entire world of resources, experts, and timely motivation needed for next-level leadership "on the go." Because audiobooks were such a benefit to my life, I released an audiobook version of my previous book, *Children's Ministry Wake Up Call,* on Amazon Audible. I have been elated to see the posts of people listening to my book while on morning strolls, bike rides, washing dishes, driving to work, and even while sitting at the beach. I have treasured each picture because these people represent my tribe. Men and women on the go who must handle a host of weighty responsibilities, yet their passion for reaching the next generation drives them to consume the content they need to be progressive leaders.

Maybe you're reading this book, and audiobooks aren't your thing, but you struggle with a book's thickness. You're not alone. Believe it or not, voluminous books tend to scare a lot of people. Kindle has calmed those fears by offering a display that reads like paper without an actual book's thickness. With adjustable front lights for indoor or outdoor use and week-long battery life, this device may be the perfect tool for those looking to avoid a sea of pages. The whole point is, **whether you love hard copy, electronic, or audiobooks, with the variety of options out there, there's no excuse why you're not reading. Find your preference and get reading today!** The truth is, we are living in the technological era. We are receiving more information at higher speeds than has ever been done before in history. With that said, the reading style will change moving forward as people's need for information goes up, but their time to do so goes down. This is the reason why *Kindle* and *Audible* have become such massively used platforms. In the future, printed books are going to be a thing of the past. Kindle, Audible, blogs, videos, podcasts, and webinars are all going to be the way forward. To embrace digital forms of reading is to embrace the future. Remember, readers are leaders, and leaders are adaptable to ensure that they stay reading.

Entrusted to Lead

From pastor to coordinator, the church has entrusted its success, growth, and development to its leaders and members. It was precisely these local leaders that inspired me to write this book. I realized that the most effective and enduring Children's Ministries are led by progressive leaders who are deliberate in their efforts to move their ministries forward. These aren't just people with a title, but people with an understanding that progression requires growth. They understand that to grow, one must acquire knowledge, and that true knowledge is birthed through action. Stated differently, success in Children's Ministry requires a progressive, forward-looking, growth mindset. Anything less amounts to the status quo and stagnation.

You will never succeed in ministry if you're not focused on becoming a progressive Children's Ministry leader. **Progressive leaders vigorously evaluate the health of their ministries by scrutinizing every area for potential improvements.** Passion fuels progressive leaders to change the world for Christ. Progressive leaders push past exhaustion, fatigue, and discouragement to reach tomorrow's generation. Progressive leaders don't ignore the gifts, talents, or resources that God has given them but channel them toward fulfilling God's call and plan! Progressive leaders take advantage of every resource – books, conferences, and practical wisdom – to enhance their ministries. They dedicate themselves to continuous improvement.

Empower yourself today through reading. Choose to rise to the occasion because your congregation needs you, the children and their families need you, and the committed volunteers rely on your expertise. You must understand how the enemy's schemes are targeting the children God has entrusted to you. You have to study and familiarize yourself with the latest trends. You must devote yourself to researching the prevailing methods of connecting with particular grade levels and how to orchestrate an environment that captures their attention and imagination. **You need to remain atop of the ever-changing best practices and be willing to apply them despite skepticism.** I pray that this chapter is waking up a sense of urgency in you to get better. One of the ways we get better is to digest and devour the wisdom God is speaking to other seasoned practitioners. You have to look at it, assess it, apply it, and bring it to the forefront.

The truth is, Progressive Children's Ministry leaders are readers, but this chapter is about more than books. It's a call to invest in yourself, and by picking up a book, you are taking a step in the right direction. It's the beginning of the journey that, if done well, can truly set you on a course to leading with excellence. But if you're not even willing to invest in yourself, then you probably shouldn't be leading in the first place. This book is for those who are serious about being progressive leaders. That's what progress is. It doesn't stay still but devotes itself to advancing, growing, and reaching for the best. **As progressive Children's Ministry leaders, we should be better tomorrow than we are today. We should be laying the foundation and groundwork to be faster, more innovative, more creative, and more efficient.**

One of my mentors told me years ago if you want to be successful, practice reading a book a week. That advice has always stayed with me even after all these years. I would be lying to you if I claimed to have lived up to that standard. But I sure do strive to get as close as I can to living out that principle. Here's why. I'm not only trying to read as many books as possible but to make a meaningful investment such that my life as a Children's Ministry influencer can be whole and lacking nothing. I want to have mastery in areas I never thought I could develop in and succeed. How about you? The reality is, all of us can succeed regardless of where you are in ministry if you are willing to put in the work to do so. Winning is no respecter of persons, and you will get there as you discover the truth and apply it. So, start to study to show yourself approved unto God. Study, study, and study some more! The more you learn, the more your appetite to discover the truth will grow. The more your desire grows, the more likely you will open the pages of that book on your bookshelf, or pull out that kindle, or listen to that audible book while driving or running errands. Read more and find yourself growing so that your department can find itself flourishing. Remember now; you will never succeed in ministry if you're not a growing leader. Leaders are readers. If you're going to win in Children's Ministry, you must commit to reading. Below are some practical reading points and practices to help you get started.

Practical Reading Points & Practices

- Choose books that you're interested in, preferably ones that could help you in areas where you may be struggling.

- Connect yourself to applicable groups and social media pages so you can stay up to date with new releases that could benefit you.

- Don't just limit yourself to books. Consider reading magazine articles and blogs as well. These resources pertain relevant advice and tools created to help you obtain next-level leadership.

- Limit distractions when you're reading. If you must multitask, choose activities that don't require a lot of brain activity and attention, for example, washing the dishes or driving while listening to an audiobook. The goal is to retain the information you receive. Try to put away extra devices that could hinder that goal.

- Take notes and highlight points that stick out to you. This is possible whether you're reading a hard copy, reading electronically, or listening to an audio version.

- Write down significant insights you receive. It's helpful to keep a notebook or journal handy so that you can keep your thoughts all in one place.

- Start a book club. Build accountability into it. Things are always more fun in community. Make it a project for your whole team, and enjoy going on a journey of discovery together.

TECH HACKS 101

◇ Start reading books through Audible and other digital resources.

◇ Subscribe to podcasts.

◇ Invest in a Kindle, Nook, or other reading tablets and use them.

◇ Subscribe to blogs and start reading content from some of your favorite thought leaders.

◇ Join and utilize online community/resource pages created to help you grow as a leader.

KEY INSIGHTS

- *A department that does not have a leader who values reading will be a department that finds itself struggling in many areas.*

- *If you consider yourself a true leader to the next generation, you must commit to learning how to be engaged in gathering good content and reading it.*

- *Leaders who fail to prioritize reading, personal growth, and continuous improvement will inevitably become frustrated and increasingly ineffective in their leadership.*

- *Reading allows you to learn from others who have already studied, achieved, or otherwise excelled in areas of ministry where you may be struggling.*

- *In reading the right books, you also need to apply the truth that you've discovered. Application is king when it comes to reading.*

- *Progressive leaders vigorously evaluate the health of their ministries by scrutinizing every area for potential improvements.*

- *You need to remain atop of the ever-changing best practices and be willing to apply them despite skepticism.*

- *One of the greatest tragedies in Children's Ministry is when a person called by God to reach the next generation for Christ completely walks away because of their lack of commitment to growth through reading.*

DISCUSSION QUESTIONS

1. What are some of the reasons or excuses that have historically prevented you from reading books or other resources that would enhance your ministry abilities?

2. Can you share an insight or other benefit that you have gained from reading that improved your leadership?

3. Have you ever justified your lack of success in a ministry area by blaming others or finding excuses instead of researching solutions or examining your role in the failure?

4. Name one or two areas where you should commit to finding resources to improve your ministry area. Research and write the titles below.

5. When it comes to reading, would you consider yourself a Progressive leader? Why or why not?

CHAPTER 2

"The only thing worse than being blind is having sight but no vision."
-Helen Keller

PROGRESSIVE LEADERS ARE VISION-DRIVEN

To be a leader is to be in the front, whether you're ready for it or not. I can still remember those early days when I was forced to lead despite being woefully unprepared to do so. A young student, fresh out of seminary, I was ready to tackle the world and become the leader God had called me to be. There was only one problem. I had absolutely no vision or even the slightest idea of where to start when it came to being a leader. I was naively confident that my love and heart for serving children and families was enough to carry any department into the future. My preconceived notions proved wrong time and time again as I faced obstacles that only a structured vision could tackle, a skill I definitely didn't possess at the time.

Unfortunately, far too many Children's ministry leaders find themselves in the exact same position. We inherit Children's Ministry positions with absolutely no goals or definition of what success means for the ministry. Leading requires sensitivity to God's voice and a keen understanding of how the church wants to reach children. So, what does the future look like in reaching children and families at your church? Even more, where is your ministry going when it comes to reaching young people? **All of us in Children's Ministry**

ought not to just be functioning from service to service, but we should be building with the future in mind. That's why I believe that **a progressive leader is vision-driven.**

Vision is God-Given

The most influential leaders take time to refine and invest in a vision. Vision is an essential element for every area of a successful life and ministry. You need a vision for the team. You need a vision for the children. You need a vision for the department. You need a vision for yourself. You need a vision for the community. You need a vision that connects with the heartbeat of God, who himself declares:

> *Remember the former things, those of long ago;*
> *I am God, and there is no other; I am God, and there is*
> *none like me.* **I make known the end from the beginning,**
> *from ancient times, what is still to come. I say, 'My purpose*
> *will stand, and I will do all that I please.'*
> - Isaiah 46:10-11 (NIV)(emphasis added).

Stated succinctly, God is the author of every prevailing vision, and every Children's Ministry leader must establish their ministries on this eternal truth. Anything less than this would be an exercise in futility! Too many, myself included, have learned the hard way that *"Unless the Lord builds the house, the builders labor in vain.* (Psalms 127: 1). Where we are now is not where we should be 10 years from now. Therefore, we must focus on the here and now while simultaneously establishing God's divine will for our ministry areas in future. It's called vision!

Vision is the ability to see the end from the beginning. The visionary leader of a Children's Ministry department will do great exploits. The unfortunate reality is that vision-driven leaders tend to be a rare breed in Children's Ministry. Far too many of us continue to operate with a "status quo" mindset, falsely believing that our "love of children" is all it takes. As much as we don't like to talk about it, it is easy to implement "weekly programming" for children that does not get them any closer to the heart of God. But today's child – more than ever – needs progressive leadership that will leave an indelible mark for Christ on their lives that this world cannot so easily erase.

Visionary Leaders Withstand Risk & Criticism

Ultimately, every leader must work toward accomplishing the vision that God has established for them and their department. Children's Ministry leaders must develop the skill and discipline to learn what God is speaking concerning their department. Good leaders are good listeners, but **result-oriented leadership must be driven by values and vision, not popular opinion.** Listening to everyone's opinion matters, but more than anything else, you've got to know what the heartbeat of God is for you and the department. You've got to understand overall where it is He is wanting to take that church when it comes to reaching children. The reality is, there may be times when God gives you a vision that may not line up with what the world expects. Sometimes carrying out a vision requires that one walks in courage and bravery as he or she challenges the status quo. This type of journey will not come without its fair share of criticism. Accordingly, progressive leaders who are vision-driven protect their mission from being negatively influenced by others' opinions.

This was especially true for Kevin McGlamery, Senior Pastor of Life Church Huntsville. He faced a decision to uproot his church from a building they had occupied for decades and was nearly paid off. Why would he do this? Because God had given him a vision. In hindsight, the decision was truly inspired and resulted in tremendous growth and diversity. Following the vision placed his church at a cross-section in the city, extending their reach and influence. But at the time, it was fraught with incredible peril, risk, and divided opinions. He chose to stay focused on the vision even when half of his senior leadership insisted this was a move that they couldn't afford. Yet Pastor Kevin remained undeterred even though the building they were to purchase was subject to zoning proceedings, which could have extinguished their ability to buy the property. He remained unwavering even though they had to live out of a mobile church for over two years as they waited for the property to become available. He remained resilient even though he risked losing half his congregation while on the road. Pastor Kevin stayed the course despite the risk. **Vision always comes with risks.** Rarely will God give you a vision that you can handle in your own strength. He's always going to provide you with a vision that exceeds your natural capacity because that's what glorifies him. **Progressive leaders are not intimidated by God-sized visions because they know the power of God-sized results.**

"If your dream in Children's Ministry doesn't scare you, it's not big enough."

It doesn't matter where you come from. It matter's where you're going. That's why vision is the difference-maker. Leadership without vision is like getting in your car and driving aimlessly. It's like running a race without knowing where the finish line is. The Bible is very clear when it comes to the consequence of having no vision.

> ### *"Where there is no vision, the people perish."*
> –Proverbs 29:18 KJV

Where there is no vision in Children's Ministry, the department suffers. Where there is no vision in Children's Ministry, there is a lack of resources. There is no better practical example of the damage of visionless leadership than the budgeting process. Inadequate budgets confront Children's Ministries across the globe. But a lot of Children's Ministries struggle precisely because their budgets are divorced from their vision. How I wish I had this knowledge during my earliest Children's Ministry positions. I still remember how confused I was when asked for my budget or my forecasted expenses for the following year. In response to this question, I floundered! I would either guestimate based on "more or less" what I spent the prior year or, worse yet, make-up a number disconnected from reality. When I look back, I realize both methods stem from a lack of vision for the ministry that I was entrusted to steward. Future budgets became a lot less daunting. My expenses and needed resources are now a natural outgrowth of already anticipated plans. Forecasting and obtaining resources is a lot less stressful when you can articulate an actionable vision, objectives, and goals for your ministry area. Stated differently, if the first time you are thinking about "next year" is when your senior pastor asks for budget numbers, then you may need to reevaluate your vision. **Vision promotes provision. Provision is attracted to the one who has a vision. When you know where you're going, you know what you need.**

Vision guides our judgment and helps us to put the necessary boundaries in place to stay the course. The first question you should ask yourself and your team when making decisions should be: is this a part of the vision? Ask this question daily. Vision determines everything when it comes to serving children and families. Vision will determine the books you read. Vision determines the conferences you attend. Vision determines who you recruit to serve on your team. Vision determines how you remodel the Children's Ministry facility. Vision determines your budget. Vision determines how you're going to advance and excel in the various ministry areas you have at your church. Vision is the difference-maker.

From Vision to Goals

Progressive leaders convert their vision into goals. As a full-time mother and wife, I am constantly weighed down with the responsibility of taking care of myself and a very needy family. I find the best way to tackle everything that needs to get done is by making daily goals. Goals help me accomplish what needs to get done by breaking it all down into bite-size pieces throughout the week. This is the same approach we should have when it comes to vision. We must break down the vision into goals. Goals help you to see, from week to week, how to reasonably achieve your ultimate vision. **Leaders who focus on goals connected to a vision will do great things for their department and the people they lead.** Think of your goals as bite-size pieces of your vision with work boots on them. Goals are of the utmost importance when it comes to any vision. Many people say they have a vision but don't have the necessary plans to support the vision.

Conversely, it is also possible for people to have goals but lack the bigger picture. This is why we must have both. Goals get you to the vision, but the vision is unachievable in the absence of goals.

People-Driven

Great leaders are equally vision-driven and people-driven. They realize that **a vision's success is inextricably linked to its ability to be understood and executed by others.** The Bible puts it this way, *"Write the revelation and make it plain on tablets **so that the herald may run with it."** (*Habakkuk 2:2)(emphasis added). In other words, the vision must be translatable to those that receive it. Your Children's Ministry vision will inevitably involve other people, so you – as the leader – must be both deliberate and intentional about effectively communicating it. Progressive Children's Ministers combine their vision with tactical action. They are results-oriented and able to confidently engage their teams with a spirit of love and humility. They don't fall victim to the temptation of either "doing-it-alone" or becoming "Children's Ministry dictators" because they lead with an understanding that *people matter.* In Children's Ministry, loving kids matter. Loving your workers' matter. And loving and connecting with parents matter. Do me a favor as you continue to read this book: remember that people matter! But we'll talk more about that in another chapter.

Progressive Children's Ministers will also be selective about the company they keep. They surround themselves with people who motivate, advise, and encourage them to pursue their God-given vision wholeheartedly. Some people will help you to push toward your vision when they sense confidence and passion in you to do so. Remember, when you have a vision, vision attracts provision. Vision also attracts people. During one of my previous Children's Ministry stints, I was pleading with my senior pastor to let me revamp one of our classrooms to make it more kid-friendly. I was absolutely convinced that we needed a space that amplified the renewed vision that I was promoting. Despite having limited resources, we were nonetheless able to create a memorable space. How? There were church members who saw the vision. They were willing to paint, do woodwork, and even create life-size characters to make the room come alive.

Martin Luther King Jr., Thomas Edison, Steve Jobs, Mother Teresa, Nelson Mandela, and the list goes on. You will be hard-pressed to name any world-changing leader that didn't have an incredible vision. These visionaries knew where they were going. Do you? As a Children's Ministry leader, do you have an end game in mind? Too many of us flounder around because we just don't know where we're going. When it comes to vision, some people don't even know where to start.

Often times you'll find that leaders lack vision because they lack exposure to visionaries. **The impossible becomes possible when we expose ourselves to other visionaries.** Visionary people are energizing and contagious. If you lack vision, consider visiting some local Children's Ministry departments and others who you admire in leadership. See what they're doing. Above all, be in prayer when it comes to vision. God must be the driving force behind our vision because that's what the Holy Spirit does. He leads us into all truth, but he can also use others. Paul implored the church of Corinth to follow him as he followed Christ. So, who do you need to follow to get those visionary wheels turning? I pride myself on having a few key people around me who I can always reach out to for inspiration. In fact, I owe some of my most outstanding achievements as a Children's Ministry influencer to insights, sparks, and inspiration that I received from God through others. **Remember, there's no shame in feeling stuck, but progressive Children's Ministry leaders don't stay there. Learn to utilize the resources around you and get the help that you need to move your Children's Ministry forward.**

"Just because every day doesn't go as planned, doesn't mean you shouldn't have a plan."

Vision is not complicated. It's really nothing more than your desired outcome, end game, and purpose concerning what you want your Children's Ministry to look like. So, what is your idea for a fruitful, successful, and thriving ministry? Have you asked yourself that question, or have you fallen victim to simply maintaining what is already in place? Have you taken time to reflect on what you want your department to look like 5, 10, or 20 years from now? Have you pondered foundational questions like: (i) how you want parents to interact in your space; (ii) how you want your department to engage with children; (iii) how you plan to implement growth; or (iv) how you plan to harmonize your vision with the overall vision of the entire church? These are all crucial questions that need consideration.

A structured strategy is vital if you're going to fulfill the overall mission. So, what's yours? I know a phenomenal leader that makes it a point to come together with his team for a strategy session every year. His first order of business is to break the ice with a fun team-building activity before starting the strategy session. Last year, he took his team to an escape room and dinner. If you don't know what an escape room is, it's a 60-minute real-life adventure game. You and your team are escorted to a themed room where you will have precisely one hour to work together to solve the mystery and escape the room. The next day, the team came together and spent the entire day going through exercises specifically designed to develop a strategy to execute their department's vision for the following year. When was the last time you and your team truly sat down together to plan a strategy around your department's vision? Please don't mistake this for an event planning meeting, which a lot of people do. I'm talking about a meeting where strategic goals are established as a roadmap to the Children's Ministry department's ultimate vision.

Can You See the Vision?

Some people choose to express their vision in unique ways. For example, vision boards are on the rise. You've heard the saying before, "a picture is worth a thousand words," and in this case, a thousand dreams. I will never forget my first vision board event. A friend invited me. The event was hosted by Tara Pickens, founder of Vision Board Inc. I was so excited. I printed off so many memorable pictures and encouraging quotes at the local Walgreens in preparation for the event. I remember gluing on a picture of my first book, *Children's Ministry Moving Forward*, as a reminder of the promise I made to create resources to help leaders worldwide move their Children's Ministries forward. I pasted a picture of my family in the right-hand corner to remind me never to lose sight of my children or marriage while pursuing my dream. Other images included newspaper clippings about my ministry and speaking engagements. Perhaps my favorite picture on the board was the one I glued right in the center, which read, *"Don't become a slave to the traditions of men."* Every day when I looked at my vision board, I was encouraged to stay the course, to be daring, bold, and never to allow any challenge, problem, or distraction to deter me from my ultimate goal.

Other people prefer to record their visions in written form. While I appreciate a more dramatic flair, I can't fault anyone from heeding the Biblical admonition, *"Then the Lord replied, 'Write the revelation and make it plain on tablets so that the herald may run with it'."* (Habakkuk 2:2). **Statistics show that people who write their goals/ vision down, are more likely to accomplish them than those who don't.** Why? For starters, writing the vision presupposes that they *have* a vision. By translating our thoughts into a written document, we are – believe it or not – already taking an active step that few are able to do. For many, the writing process forces one to distill, consolidate, or organize their thoughts. This process alone makes the vision more permanent and capable of review by the author and other sources of accountability. One study, called "The

Gender Gap and Goal Setting," examined both preferences when recording one's vision. Participants in the study were asked to rate the question, "My goal is so vividly described in written form (including pictures, photos, drawings, etc.) that I could literally show it to other people and they would know exactly what I'm trying to achieve. From the study, only 20% of participants said that their goals were 'Always' written down this vividly. Vividly describing your goals in written form is strongly associated with goal success, and people who vividly describe or picture their goals are anywhere from 1.2 to 1.4 times more likely to successfully accomplish their goals than people who don't.

My husband loves writing his goals down. At the end of each year, he spends time in prayer to seek God's will for several keystone areas of his life for the following year: spiritual maturity, marriage, parenting, professional development, health/fitness, finances, and emotional wellness. Following this, he will set an overarching goal for the year (e.g., create memorable experiences for the kids), but he will also break them down into monthly goals (e.g., visit a museum in January). I find his goal documents on the printer, in the bathroom, and scattered in other random places throughout the house. For him, the entire process: prayer, research, writing, printing, and reviewing becomes a reinforcing cycle of strategic execution. While he hasn't hit every goal with 100% accuracy, he is undoubtedly further along than he would be without them.

The whole point is, GET SPECIFIC WITH YOUR GOALS! This is perhaps one of the most important courses of action one should take if they ever hope to have any success in reaching their vision. Even still, there are so many Children's Ministry leaders who don't do it. Thousands of studies have proven that those who get specific with their goals are more likely to achieve them than those who set broader ones. In her book, *9 Things Successful People Do Differently*, Heidi Grant Halvorson suggests implementing a strategy called "mental contrasting" as a way to strengthen one's commitment. The technique requires one to imagine a desired future and the rewards of attaining that future, coupled with the obstacles that may hinder that future. In other words, it strengthens one's resolve to act on the goals they have set by visualizing the pros and the cons they may face on the path to get there. For example, suppose you set a goal to provide programming to equip parents better. In that case, you visualize how amazing it would be to provide an event that genuinely connects with parents' hearts and makes them feel better equipped to be the spiritual guides in their own homes. Then, you reflect on the obstacles or the pitfalls that may get in the way of you doing that effectively. For example, dealing with parents' already swamped schedules or providing the right type of content parents feel they need. The mental contrasting encourages you to take the necessary steps to avoid the cons and successfully achieve your goal. Bottom line, taking the appropriate time to reflect on the future you desire mentally, and the hurdles you will have to face to get there will help you to catch the drive and ambition you need to achieve that goal.

The beauty of vision boards, written goals, and mental contrasting is that they help you better see or anticipate your vision's execution. If I'm exercising with a vision in mind, I see a picture of a leaner, fitter, healthier Esther. The image seems all the more accessible when I know what I'm working towards. The Apostle Paul puts it this way in the book of 1 Corinthians:

> *Run in such a way as to get the prize. Everyone who competes in a game goes into strict training. They do it to get a crown that will not last, but we do it to get a crown that will last forever. Therefore I do not run like someone running aimlessly; I do not fight like a boxer beating the air. No, I strike a blow to my body and make it my slave so that after I have preached to others, I myself will not be disqualified for the prize.*
>
> - 1 Corinthians 9:24b-27

Children's Ministry leaders who are vision-driven keep their eyes on the prize; they don't run aimlessly, but they discipline their bodies so that they might obtain the prize of seeing their vision fulfilled. Christ himself bore the cross because of the glory on the other side. In other words, Christ was able to endure the pain of the cross because he kept his eyes on the future glory (i.e., the vision fulfilled). His focus should be a genuinely noteworthy example for all of us. In short, **vision can help sustain us when things get hard.** We see the same principle in the life of Abraham. In Genesis 12, we witness the powerful encounter between Abraham and his creator. Despite being advanced in age and married to a woman who was well-past her childbearing years, God told Abraham that he would have a son of his own. Yet the beauty of this moment is in the visual or **vision** that God gives Abraham:

> *He took him outside and said, "Look up at the sky and count the stars — if indeed you can count them." Then he said to him, "So shall your offspring be." Abram believed the Lord, and he credited it to him as righteousness.*
>   - Genesis 14:4-5 (NIV).

I often ponder that critical moment in Abraham's faith journey. Our Heavenly Father understood that Abraham needed to *see* the promise. It wasn't enough to tell him that his descendants would be innumerable; he needed Abraham to walk outside and picture it! Abraham needed this visual because it would be a *long* time before the fulfillment of this promise. But I suppose that is why God gifted Abraham with such a powerful reminder. Every time he looked up at the stars, he remembered the promises of God. This vision sustained him even when his circumstances couldn't be farther from that vision. He and Sarah grew older and older with each passing year, but he had to cling to that promised vision. I believe God gives us vision, so we know what we're pressing toward, especially when our current reality doesn't live up to it.

Vision inspires. Know that if you're going to be progressive in Children's Ministry, you have to spend time with God, spend time with your church leadership, spend time with your team, and

WRITE THE VISION! **Identify what you're going to do with what God has called you to do and then, be willing to pay the price.** Remind yourself that vision is never accomplished without a driven understanding that all things are possible to them that believe. As a progressive leader, you must continue to cultivate and steward your God-given vision if you ever hope to extend the reach and impact of your ministry to children and families.

TECH HACKS 101

◇ Embrace new models of technology in documenting your vision.

◇ Use smart devices like Alexa, Echo, etc.... to help remind you of your goals.

◇ Create a digital vision board. Make the graphic the screensaver on your computer, laptop, and smartphone.

◇ Start listening to podcasts from some of your favorite visionaries.

◇ Leverage digital platforms to keep your vision in the forefront. For example, you can frequently cite the vision in your social media posts, etc.

KEY INSIGHTS

- *All of us in Children's Ministry ought not to just be functioning from service to service, but we should be building with the future in mind.*

- *Result-oriented leadership must be driven by values and vision, not popular opinion.*

- *Progressive leaders are not intimidated by God-sized visions because they know the power of God-sized results.*

- *Vision promotes provision. Provision is attracted to the one who has a vision. When you know where you're going, you know what you need.*

- *Leaders who focus on goals connected to a vision will do great things for their department and the people they lead.*

- *The success of a vision is inextricably linked to its ability to be understood and executed by others.*

- *The impossible becomes possible when we expose ourselves to other visionaries.*

- *There's no shame in feeling stuck, but progressive Children's Ministry leaders don't stay there. Learn to utilize the resources around you and get the help that you need to move your Children's Ministry forward.*

- *A structured strategy is vital if you're going to fulfill the overall mission.*

- *People who write their goals or vision down are more likely to get them done than those who don't.*

- *Vision can help sustain us when things get hard.*

- *Identify what you're going to do with what God has called you to do and then, be willing to pay the price.*

DISCUSSION QUESTIONS

1. Have you invested time to seek God for a vision for your Children's Ministry? If so, what insights have you gleaned? If not, under what or whose vision were you operating?

2. Have you effectively communicated your vision for the Children's Ministry to others? What are some ways to translate your vision into action plans that others can understand and follow?

3. How have you responded when your vision hits roadblocks or criticism?

4. Is your Children's Ministry budgeting process consistent with your vision? Are there other areas of your ministry that you could better align with your vision?

5. Who are some visionaries that you admire? What makes their visions so compelling?

6. What are some of the ways you can write, document, or otherwise "see" your vision?

7. How has vision sustained you through difficult or challenging times in ministry?

CHAPTER 3

*"It is amazing what you can accomplish, if you do not care
who gets the credit"*
-Harry S. Truman

PROGRESSIVE LEADERS ARE TEAM-ORIENTED

Andrew Carnegie is credited with the saying, "Teamwork is the
ability to work together toward a common vision. It is the fuel
that allows common people to attain uncommon results." **With all
the work that lay before us to reach the next generation for
Christ, it is unfathomable to believe that greatness can be
achieved alone.** On the contrary, everyone serving in Children's
Ministry as leaders, directors, coordinators, and general overseers
must work as teams. As cliché' as it sounds, teamwork really does make
the dream work. For any of us to do something truly significant, we
have to think beyond ourselves. In Children's Ministry, we must get
better at building teams. With the vast number of churches growing
into megachurches and hundreds of children gathering on church
campuses across America (and around the world), no one person can
effectively run a dynamic Children's Ministry. That's why I believe
a progressive Children's Ministry leader is team-oriented.

Principles of Team-Oriented Leadership

The progressive leader who is team-oriented understands that they can't do it all by themselves. These leaders embrace certain truths that revolutionize both how they see themselves and how they relate to others. As we have already covered, **you may be well-read, researched, or be a tremendous visionary but a lack of people skills will significantly hinder the success of your Children's Ministry department**. A leader's impact on a project, organization, or even a movement cannot be understated. I have seen far too many well-resourced, staffed, and competent teams fail to achieve their objectives because of ill-equipped leaders. But I have also seen incredible results achieved by what started out as poorly-resourced teams, staffed with ill-suited members, all because of a phenomenal leader at the helm. The point is simple: leadership matters, but leaders don't exist apart from their team. There are key principles that leaders must implement if they wish to move toward growth when it comes to dynamic team-oriented leadership. These principles must serve as the framework for every leader if they want to move toward success.

Principle #1- Know you. To lead others, you must know yourself. **You should always know your strengths and weaknesses before recruiting others to serve on a team.** You should know without a shadow of a doubt "who you are" and "what you bring to the table" to effectively lead a team. It is often difficult to see value in others when you are blind to your own. In my journey as a leader, I have felt the pressure to be someone I am not. It was hard for me to lean into my strengths or even notice them because I was too busy overcompensating for my weaknesses instead of allowing those whom God had sent me to carry the load. Children's Ministry leaders must get to know who they are, accept who they are-battle scars and all, and love who they are before leading others. I have personally witnessed the catastrophic ramifications of leaders who don't know who they are. When you don't know who you are, you operate from a place of uncertainty and insecurity, and when that happens, everybody loses! Trust me, I know. You will never be successful in leading teams if you zero all your energy on being good at something that is not your strength. The truth is, you're not good at everything, and that's okay! Diversity is the beauty of teams. So, do you know who you are?

More importantly, have you embraced who you are and who you are not? Learning who you are requires you to go on a journey of self-discovery. It requires you to take an honest look in the mirror and identify your strengths and weaknesses. I find inviting others into your journey of self-discovery can prove extremely beneficial if done the right way. Be bold enough to seek the opinions of trusted individuals who love you enough to tell you the truth concerning your strengths and weaknesses, and no cheating! Something I've discovered over the years is that there is always someone out there who will support your truth, even when it's a lie! It is natural to cling to those people because they tell us what we want to hear. **I have also discovered that some of those same people are watching you fail when they can help you but remain silent because you insist on doing everything yourself.** We will talk more about this later on in this chapter.

Principle #2- Get to know people. Progressive leaders also know that their success hinges on recruiting, getting to know, and valuing their Children's Ministry co-laborers. **Never underestimate the retention power of relationships.** It's also worth getting to know people in your church whether they serve in the Children's Ministry or not. Your goal is to expose yourself to others who could *potentially* help in the Children's Ministry. This is not the only reason you invest in relationships, but it is a great way to discover those God has already called to help you in the ministry. Remember, **if you aren't intentional when it comes to branching out and getting to know others, you will significantly limit your ability to build a team.** Progressive leaders who are team-oriented don't restrict themselves exclusively to the Children's Ministry department because they understand to get and keep people, you have to know people.

This truth was amplified in my own life several years ago when I was called to serve at a church in the Chicagoland area. Despite a slew of applicants, I received a call from the senior pastor inviting me to serve their children and families. Not only was I welcomed with a healthy list of roles and responsibilities, but I also inherited a skeleton crew. During that season, I realized that it is well worth the time and effort to invest in people and relationships, irrespective of their intent to serve in my ministry. I participated in things that had nothing to do with Children's Ministry. I showed up to events when I didn't feel like it. I even signed up for a midweek Bible study, which, to my surprise, only included the elderly members of the church, all to build relationships and discover new people. In my heart, I had very little hope of recruiting viable workers from the weekly Bible Study because very few senior citizens get too excited about Children's Ministry. Nonetheless, I stayed and enjoyed the fellowship, accountability, and beautiful relationships that did blossom from it.

One of those cherished relationships was with a beautiful soul named Julie. As always, the season came around when it was time to fill my Sunday School roster for the year. God was so faithful that year. We had some fabulous people recommit to serve. But even in God's faithfulness, I would be lying if I didn't say that my heart sunk a little every time I saw the empty space where the second-grade leader's name was supposed to be, but I trusted God even as the clock ticked away. Maybe you've felt that way before. Did I mention that no one accepted the call to serve after all my relation-building efforts, except one person? With only two weeks of summer remaining, I wasn't sure what to do with the second grade class for the Fall Semester, but then it happened. I checked my office mailbox, usually full of junk mail in the summer, but this time there was only a little sheet of paper curled up in the back. To my surprise, it was a note from my new friend Julie volunteering to serve as a second grade Sunday School teacher. Not only did Julie become a fabulous Sunday School teacher, but she also became an invaluable part of our Children's Ministry Leadership Team. This experience encouraged me **never to put limits on God or his ability to call people from the most unexpected places to help us.** Through that experience, I learned that getting to know people is absolutely a time investment, but a worthy one.

It's important to know *who* you're serving alongside. It's important to know *who* you're inviting to join the team. Remember, when building a team, no two groups are alike. The approach you take at one church may need to be significantly different for the next body. These changes represented "growing pains" for me. Having had a certain degree of success in my first ministry position, I mistakenly believed I could just "copy and paste" my leadership style into the next role. But I learned the hard way that leadership is not a one-size-fits-all proposition, and my new team had very different expectations for their Children's Ministry leader. We can recycle some of our best ideas and approaches, but we must do so with a keen understanding of who we are to lead. The point: **progressive leaders tailor their leadership style to the teams they serve.**

"If you don't believe you can retain and recruit workers, you won't retain and recruit workers."

Principle #3- Embrace differences. When you bring a team together, you must understand that teams work best with multiple talents and giftings. Differences strengthen teams. If we were all the same, any of us would be replaceable. Building teams that embrace differences can be a challenging endeavor. Whether we like it or not, we tend to gravitate toward people who are more like us. The truth is, it's easier for us to get along with people who are just like us, but if we're going to build a dynamic ministry for children, then we must learn how to work with different people. Ultimately, you're going to have to learn to appreciate what you bring to the table, as discussed in principle #1, while also genuinely celebrating the giftings of others. Recognizing others' strengths will become particularly important when delegating tasks to team members. If you hear nothing more in this chapter, hear this: **just because you're the leader doesn't mean you have to do everything! As the leader, you're responsible for ensuring things get done, but you don't have to be the person who's doing it.** Thriving Children's Ministries of tomorrow are going to have to think as teams! Remember, alone, we can do little, but together we can do so much more.

Embracing Diversity in Teams

When it comes to building teams, diversity is the future. There are countless benefits of having a diverse team. Diverse groups are known to be more creative, productive, and even profitable. They're less prone to struggle with affinity bias and suboptimal decision-making biases. One popular known bias is referred to as *Groupthink*, a process where group norms and patterns cause well-intentioned group members to agree with each other resulting in deeply flawed decision making. Even though building diverse teams may be challenging, the benefits of differing perspectives far outweigh those initial challenges. In fact, according to a McKinsey study, after examining diversity in the workplace concluded that 35%

of teams that were ethnically diverse were more likely to outperform industry norms. If our goal is truly to reach children of all ethnicities and backgrounds, progressive leaders must build diverse teams that represent everybody. I hear so many leaders say they want diversity in their ministries. Still, most of their leadership teams are comprised of people who are culturally, ethnically, socioeconomically, geographically, and generally identical in every way. God's heart for diversity is readily visible throughout the pages of Scripture. From the Gospel's proclamation in various tongues in Acts 2 to the multicultural congregation worshiping before the throne in Revelations, His heart for all nations is unambiguously clear. Despite the vision of every tribe, tongue, and nation worshipping in one accord, this picture is rarely realized today. Unfortunately, Sunday continues to be the most segregated day of the week. But the real question for all Progressive Children's Ministry Leaders is whether our churches reflect the diversity of the communities we serve?

While there have been remarkable strides in the area of diversity and inclusion, I believe the most powerful changes will only come through the next generation. Therefore, we – as Children's Ministry leaders – must live and model these truths. As a Black woman, one of the most rewarding aspects of my ministry has been to serve in a cross-cultural capacity. By leading lessons and regularly teaching predominately White children, I am not only imparting the Word of God but serving as a counter-stereotypical example of a Black woman. My sincere hope is that when my children interact with other cultures or people groups, they will not so quickly result to fear, criminalization, or rejection. When they see a Black man, I hope they see my husband, their Sunday School teacher, instead of the hyper-criminalized image so pervasive in the modern media. Exposure to positive Black figures may mean that they avoid the historical baggage that their forefathers carried. It may mean that we all, together, grow one step closer to the picture of the diverse, loving, and spirit-led body of Christ that He called us to become.

Progressive leaders must understand that it's the process of doing life together that cultivates a heart of empathy

and authentic concern for other people groups. It's natural to be blind to others' legitimate concerns and struggles when we are ignorant about their experiences. This is why diversity in leadership is paramount! Having diverse leaders and voices speaking to issues that don't line up with your personal world view or frame of reference is vital if all are to be reached. When sensitive issues or historical pains erupt, churches that operate with diverse teams can better anticipate reactions and minister more effectively. Why? Because these leaders sit on diverse teams with more varied insights and experiences to help them navigate these emotionally-charged situations. At the end of the day, if our primary objective is Christ being born and developed in all, then we have to recognize the enemy's attack is to sow seeds of discord among God's people. We also need to remember that our enemy comes to kill, steal, and destroy, and a house divided against itself cannot stand. This same tactic is wreaking havoc on the unity of believers across the globe. But like Christ, we can purpose ourselves to tear down the walls of hostility because there's one church, one baptism, and one God. Yes, it's good that brothers dwell together in unity, but this goal is often conditional on acts of healing, forgiveness, and reconciliation. Don't be a leader who leads in an echo chamber. Progressive Leaders who are team-oriented will move forward with diversity in mind.

Delegation

Team-oriented leaders understand the absolute need to clarify roles and responsibilities. **When different people show up, confusion will enter the room or take over the department entirely when roles and responsibilities are not clearly defined.** Knowing the roles and responsibilities of those on your team helps you to delegate well. Building teams and delegating is not a new concept in Children's Ministry, but there are still so many Children's Ministry leaders out there who fail to do so. In my years serving in Children's Ministry, here's what I've discovered.

Leaders who insist on doing everything find themselves burning out. What's worse, those leaders often find themselves plagued with bitterness. They say inappropriate things about the senior pastor or other leaders out of their personal hurt. Please know one of the enemy's most significant lies is that your senior pastor doesn't care about the Children's Ministry. Of course, he or she cares! They cared so much; they entrusted the job to you! Don't allow frustration to cloud your judgment regarding those serving alongside you in the same battle to win souls for Christ. The enemy feeds off of confusion. Don't give him a chance! Choose to be a progressive leader that is team-oriented. Know the roles and responsibilities you're going to need even before you get the people you need to execute them.

"God himself said, it's not good for man to be alone, so why are you trying to do it all by yourself?"

Leaders who fail to plan for their support adequately are the most at risk of burning out while bearing the weight of the ministry alone. Even Moses was on the brink of burnout. When you think about it, can you blame him? After coming to Egypt, navigating the ten plagues, and leading a multitude of God's people through the wilderness, a little burnout was inevitable. Undoubtedly, he could handle a lot, but there are limits. Despite his supernatural support, Moses nonetheless struggled with the one-man-band syndrome. He alone was resolving every case, controversy, and challenge that confronted an entire nation. It wasn't until his father-in-law paid a visit that he realized he need not bear this burden alone.

> *"When his father-in-law saw all Moses was doing for the people, he said, "What is this you are doing for the people? Why do you alone sit as judge, while all these people stand around you from morning till evening?" Moses answered him, "Because the people come to me to seek God's will. Whenever they have a dispute, it is brought to me, and I decide between the parties and inform them of God's decrees and instructions." Moses' father-in-law replied, "What you are doing is not good. You and these people who come to you will only wear yourselves out. The work is too heavy for you; you cannot handle it alone."*
>
> *-Exodus 18:14-18 NIV*

Just like Moses, we too can fall victim to the one-man-band syndrome if we're not careful. It is not uncommon for Children's Ministry leaders to feel responsible for *every* aspect of the Children's Ministry department and thus take on most of the load. There are several reasons for this phenomenon. One cause is the unrealistic expectations of leadership imposed upon us by other members of our faith community. We also become so accustomed to leading on our own terms for so long that we build up an unconscious aversion to any other way. Such a mindset may be especially dangerous because it can cause us to reject innovative ideas and the people that offer them.

Progressive leaders don't merely record their vision, but they also take time to evaluate what roles are needed to execute that vision. No leader is good at everything. Every leader has something to offer. But no leader has everything to offer! Everybody has a weakness, and everybody has a strength. It is vital when building a healthy team that you connect people to roles associated with their strengths. Remember, everyone has something to offer. Take the time to learn people's strengths. Then place them in the right position. Only then will people be able to provide their best service to the Children's Ministry department.

Finally, progressive leaders aren't afraid of constructive feedback. **No matter how you try to flip the coin, feedback is necessary for excellence in ministry.** Rejecting feedback limits your department and what you're ultimately able to accomplish. Feedback is like the breakfast of champions. There is someone on your team who can see what you can't. There is someone on your team who can do what you can't. There is someone on your team who can supply precisely what the team or church needs. Remember, alone you can do little, but together you can do much. Teamwork is vital for success in Children's Ministry. You have to build a culture that celebrates teamwork. Basketball legend Michael Jordan once said, "talent wins games, but teamwork wins championships." Be smart enough to accept the truth that someone's assignment is to help you, particularly in areas where you're weak. Together, we can do so much more for the kingdom. So, make the investment to become a progressive leader that is team-oriented.

TECH HACKS 101

◇ Consider utilizing file-sharing software like Sharepoint, Google docs, Dropbox, etc., to assist in monitoring progress on projects, clarifying roles and responsibilities, etc.

◇ Leverage digital technology for team growth and development. Attend virtual conferences, webinars, and trainings with your team.

◇ Communicate with your team through group texting apps. (Be leery of over-communicating in these applications, so your team members don't begin to write off important announcements.)

◇ Pair technology with team building activities. Make this fun! Incorporate virtual icebreakers, online team building games, and more.

◇ Use a variety of different digital communication channels to stay connected with your team.

KEY INSIGHTS

- *With all the work that lay before us to reach the next generation for Christ, it is unfathomable to believe that greatness can be achieved alone.*

- *You may be well-read, researched, or be a tremendous visionary, but you will severely hinder your Children's Ministry department if you lack the necessary people skills.*

- *You should always know your own strengths and weaknesses before recruiting others to serve on a team.*

- *Some people are watching you fail when they can help you but remain silent because you insist on doing everything yourself.*

- *If you aren't intentional when it comes to branching out and getting to know others, you will significantly limit your ability to build a team.*

- *Never put limits on God or his ability to call people from the most unexpected places to help us.*

- *Progressive leaders tailor their leadership style to the teams they serve.*

- *Just because you're the leader doesn't mean you have to do everything! As the leader, you're responsible for ensuring that it's done, but you don't have to be the person who does it.*

- *When it comes to building teams, diversity is the future.*

- *Progressive leaders must understand that it's the process of doing life together that cultivates a heart of empathy and authentic concerns for other people groups.*

- *When different people show up, confusion will enter the room or take over the department entirely when roles and responsibilities are not clarified.*

- *No matter how you try to flip the coin, feedback is necessary for excellence in ministry.*

DISCUSSION QUESTIONS

1. What are your strengths and weaknesses in ministry? Identify one unbiased person you will commit to getting feedback from to help you on your self-discovery journey.

2. Are you apart of teams where differences are embraced or avoided? Explain.

3. Does your leadership team reflect the diversity of the surrounding community? If not, what are some ways to further promote diversity and inclusion on your team?

4. Have you ever been a victim of the one-man-band syndrome? If so, what are some of the reasons that caused you to do it alone? What will you become intentional at doing in the future to ensure you don't go at it alone the next time?

5. Have you ever experienced burnout in Children's Ministry? What caused you to feel this way? Name one thing you will do moving forward to prevent burnout in your own life and ministry.

CHAPTER 4

"For every minute spent organizing, an hour is earned."
–Benjamin Franklin

PROGRESSIVE LEADERS ARE ORGANIZERS

Given the expanding responsibilities, evolving ministry dynamics, and enhanced communication expectations, today's Children's Ministry leaders can no longer operate like in times past. A Progressive Children's Ministry leader needs to be an organizer. **Children's Ministry leaders must learn how to organize their personal lives and the ministry departments they steward.** The unfortunate reality is that many Children's Ministry leaders are messy, unorganized, and their spaces are filled with junk. Instead of improving in this area, far too many leaders carry it as a badge of honor and a byproduct of being a Children's Minister. Well, it's time to clean off that desk. Go through that pile of who knows what that's been sitting there for months! We're about to clean house because progressive Children's Ministry leaders understand that when their lives and ministries are unorganized, it affects their productivity. Ready or not, this chapter is going to give you nine steps to becoming more organized, which will help you to thrive in ministry and excel in what you're doing for children and families. So, grab your broom, and let's go!

#1: *Write it Down*

Learning to write things down is one of the most straightforward steps you can take to enhance your ministry. You'd be amazed at the number of Children's Ministry leaders that have a vast breadth of responsibilities on their plates but somehow try to track them with nothing more than their memories. I learned this truth the hard way years ago! Four weeks after having my first child, I prematurely rushed back to lead our annual vacation bible school right when it was scheduled to start. Talk about a disaster. The church secretary watched the baby while I danced and presented on stage. Most of the breakout sessions were spent with me frantically tethered to a breast pump with mere moments to spare before it was time to go back to the stage. I was the epitome of a chicken with her head cut off. Despite multiple reminders, I couldn't remember anything, including the announcement to be made every day that week! It was such a nightmare! Let's just say I learned a few lessons from this experience. First, don't rush back to work after giving birth to a human being! But more importantly, it's a good idea to write things down.

Here's the deal, we forget things! It's completely natural. In fact, the older we get, the easier it is to forget. So, to ensure that you're not missing out on any of your responsibilities, it's better to make it a habit to write things down. Don't underestimate the power of a pen and paper when it comes to remembering things. Truthfully, people can be unforgiving when you fail to deliver on your commitments, and saying "I forgot" is rarely an acceptable or satisfactory excuse. Put differently, *"But let your 'Yes' be "Yes,' and your 'No,' 'No.'"* (Matthew 5:37a, NKJV). Remember, we are serving the church of Christ, not perfect people. When people feel disregarded, and feelings get hurt, all manner of confusion can break out. Recording and writing things down serve as a reminder of what needs to get done. A notebook and a pencil are much better than random ideas floating around in our heads. Trust me! As a leader, you never want to garner a reputation of being unreliable. One easy solution is to record tasks immediately on your phone. This way, you note the task and set a reminder in advance of the job that needs attention. There are various applications such as Evernote, Todoist, Dropbox, and more that can assist in recording your to-do's on your phone in a fast and organized way. Also, don't sleep on other smart devices that could help you keep track of your responsibilities. Smart devices such as Amazon Alexa/ Echo, Google Assistant, and Apple HomePod, just to name a few, are great ways to store everyday tasks you don't want to forget. The great thing about these devices is that many can integrate and sync with organization apps, helping to keep everything you need to know in one place. Remember, if you want to be organized, whether you're a pen and paper or a digital guru, learn to practice the art of recording and writing things down.

#2: Mind the Deadline

The journey to becoming more organized includes scheduling and adhering to deadlines. These seemingly simple disciplines can revolutionize your efficiency and effectiveness. Time is valuable. As a Children's Ministry leader, you've got to remember that time is one of your most precious resources. With mounting to-do list pressure, you must prioritize and allocate time toward doing what needs to be done. In short, progressive leaders don't waste time! Many of us have experienced the constant pull of ministry, which may cause us to miscalculate our deadlines and priorities. I use to be notorious for saying "yes" to every request made of me. When you are in ministry, there are many other leaders, parents, and different ministry areas that vie for your time and attention. Studies show it takes 25 to 40 percent longer to get a job done when you're simultaneously trying to work on other projects. In the absence of a defined schedule with clear deadlines, it is easy to fall victim to every request. On one occasion, I had so overextended myself that I failed to prepare for the service on Sunday adequately. I essentially added more and more to my plate without calculating the corresponding time investment. Overcommitment is not an uncommon mistake for leaders, especially when they don't operate with deadlines in mind. But **organized leaders, set and stick to reasonable deadlines, which result in a better understanding of what they do (or don't) have time to accomplish.**

Progressive leaders recognize that being organized goes hand in hand with productivity. Remember, if you want to be productive in ministry, you need to embrace and execute scheduling and deadlines. Progressive leaders insist on making and keeping schedules to prioritize time allocation from days to weeks to months. Going forward, choose to be as productive as possible in your ministry to children by setting and sticking to deadlines.

"Children's Ministry departments with no organizational structure will be limited in their growth."

#3 Prevent Procrastination

This brings us to number three. Progressive leaders don't procrastinate! Procrastination is something that can sneak up on you in a minute if you're not careful. Delay, avoidance, exhaustion, whatever the cause may be, result from procrastination. Many leaders needlessly suffer because it is easy to avoid responsibility, but this delay can cause you and your department to suffer. The longer you wait to get something done in ministry, the more difficult it will be to get it done. The problem will only compound when we fail to take care of our responsibilities at the appropriate time. Ironically, if you want your ministry experience to be less stressful, then completing your activities at the scheduled time will help to alleviate much of your stress. The goal is to stay focused. Staying on task can be difficult, especially when you work in an open workspace where people can just pop their heads in at any moment. It's easy for one quick comment or joke to snowball into a full-fledged conversation that sucks up a large chunk of your day. Trust me. I've been there. I've talked to multiple colleagues who have shared their tips and tricks on protecting their productivity from investing in noise-canceling headphones, signs, cones, and other items that serve as do not disturb signals to those around them. The whole point is to protect your productivity so you can complete tasks on time.

Doing things at the appropriate time not only benefits you but your team as well. In essence, procrastination is nothing more than waiting until the last minute. So, while you may be comfortable burning the midnight oil, it may be wreaking havoc on your Children's Ministry workers who don't operate well under those same standards. **Last-minute notices force all of the Children's Ministry workers involved in the department to scramble. The result is a suboptimal performance and less effective programming for children**. Know this, well-intentioned workers who are constantly up against a wall will leave. Don't let that happen. With nothing more than a little preplanning on behalf of the leader, the department can be significantly more impactful for your team and the children you serve. Organization is essential. Procrastinators tend to be unorganized. Conversely, the more organized you become, the less likely you or your team will want or need to procrastinate.

#4 Everything in its Proper Place

A progressive leader understands and appreciates the fact that everything needs a place. Trust me, it helps! Make sure your ministry department has a structural model where everything has a place. With everything on your plate as a children's ministry leader, it's easy to get lost in the busyness and start leaving things everywhere! I know it may seem easier to throw that item in a convenient spot where it doesn't belong for the short term, but it will ultimately cost you money, time, and a level of frustration down the road when you have no idea where it is. **An organized department means keeping and returning items to their proper place. Organized leaders maintain order by storing, labeling, and managing their things properly.** High performers, in ministry and beyond, tend to be masters of organization. They don't waste time searching for needed tools, documents, or resources because they make it a habit to put things where they belong.

Part of maintaining order and organization is making space. Let's talk about all things clutter! An organized leader declutters regularly. It's easy to collect stuff, and before you know it, your office looks like an episode of Hoarders! Children's Ministry leaders must take the necessary time to organize their materials and affairs. No matter how much we wish it did, our stuff will not organize itself. It needs to be periodically gone through as you accumulate more ministry resources. No storage space can be excluded from this process. Your closets, trunks, garages, decks, and any other secret box, bin, or drawer where you stuff things. Why? Because a Children's Ministry leader's life can be overrun by stuff very quickly. It's as if "hoarder" were a requirement in our job descriptions. I get it! Many of us have had no other choice and have feared getting rid of things that may prove beneficial to us later because of limited budgets. We collect tons of stuff with the genuine belief that it will be useful in the future. But how many of us put that same stuff in a storage container, never to be seen again. How many of us have found that our offices also serve as the donation bin for all of the used, broken, or dusty toys, books, and games that church families no longer want? **Don't let your Children's Ministry become the dumping ground for everything that well-intentioned people don't want in their homes anymore!** You don't want to have to spend your own time and resources to rent a truck to haul all of that stuff out just because you have a problem saying no to donations. Never be afraid to decline a donation your department just doesn't need. Stop letting clutter slow down your productivity. If you don't need it, call it junk and get rid of it! We've all been there one time or another. My advice is to GET RID OF IT!

#5 Pick & Purge with a Purpose

Only keep what you need. If we're going to organize our space, we have to embrace the fact that there are some things we're just not going to use anymore, and that's okay. Keeping things that you don't need is going to affect you and your level of productivity. Remember, more stuff means more clutter! This is true in ministry and life. Just ask my car! If you aspire to be a Progressive Children's Ministry leader, then be willing to retain only those items and resources you genuinely NEED that have a specific purpose in your ministry. Choose to live organized lives. Choose only to keep what you really need or want (and I say the word "want" with caution). Choose to be a leader who is committed and capable of getting rid of stuff.

Progressive Children's Ministry leaders know how to purge with a purpose. Do what you can to get rid of stuff you're not going to use anymore. Less stuff means less clutter. But consider giving your things to other Children's Ministry leaders. As we all know, one man's junk is another man's treasure. Remember, there's always another church that could use that old VBS kit, Styrofoam character, or prop to make their space come alive. If you're able, send stuff that you're not going to use to overseas ministries. The whole point is to find a way to get rid of stuff, but let's do so in a way that advances the Kingdom. Several churches will pool, share, and recycle resources. I highly encourage you to form those cooperative relationships with other Children's Ministry leaders. Not only do they save money, time, and resources, but they also serve as a constant reminder to review, recycle, and purge your storage spaces.

#6 Beware the Bargain

Stay away from bargains! Now before you demand a public stoning, hear me out. Many Children's Ministry leaders have become extremely good at collecting junk in the form of bargain shopping. After you've removed the things you don't need, will you replace them with something else when you see the next sale? Children's Ministry leaders get themselves in significant trouble when it comes to bargains. Now, seeing a deal in and of itself isn't a bad thing when you have a plan in place. So how do you avoid impulse bargain buying? After you have a vision, goals, and a plan, write down exactly what you need and limit your purchases to those items. **Progressive organized leaders don't give into advertising.** Sales only produce more clutter. Children's Ministry leaders need to learn what they need ahead of time and then discipline themselves to buy nothing more!

"Clutter represents indecisions. Make a decision and clear the clutter!"

#7 Delegate & Celebrate

As we have discussed before, delegation is essential to effective teamwork, and organized leaders delegate responsibly. Progressive Children's Ministry leaders don't allow themselves to be overburdened by too many responsibilities, meetings, and deadlines. Instead, they consistently assess their teams and delegate tasks to teammates that are just as (if not more) capable of carrying out those tasks. While some people may accuse these leaders of delegating away their jobs, the reality is that these leaders have become organizational masters. They understand that they can better focus on value-adding activities and objectives by delegating everything else to their team members. There is no shame in sharing the ministry load with those around you, provided you delegate correctly.

I've observed many leaders who have struggled with delegation throughout my years in ministry because of an unhealthy preoccupation with doing everything themselves. Many of them were motivated by a fear of rejection, which prevented them from even asking for help. They reasoned themselves out of even asking for support because they assumed that people didn't have time, were too busy, or otherwise weren't interested in helping with Children's Ministry. In essence, they said "no" on someone else's behalf. On the other hand, we should always be careful not to over-delegate either. I have witnessed serious fights break out when a Children's Ministry worker felt that she bore the Children's Ministry's entire load while the leader sat idly by, unwilling to lift a finger. Organized leaders strategically delegate to their teams because they know and value them for their contributions. Your **delegation considers both roles and responsibilities, coupled with your team's strengths, weaknesses, and capacity.** Finally, leaders should never use bullying or manipulation in their delegation. Remember, excellent leaders drive, motivate, and inspire outstanding teams.

#8 Optimize Your Schedule

An integral part of organizing your day is just knowing yourself and your most productive times. Some people are morning people. Some people are evening people. Some people are after lunch people. So, what are you? Children's Ministry leaders must reserve their optimal hours when they're at their best for the most challenging and complex tasks because those tasks require more brainpower. When you're tired, go ahead and stick to more manageable tasks. **Progressive leaders organize their days around their optimal hours.** They also think about and sequence those tasks that are theirs and someone else's and plan accordingly. While you're working on tasks A and B, consider giving another person tasks C and D. That way, by the time you need tasks C and D, it will be complete. Super organized people think through the necessary sequencing and outsourcing to maximize their productivity. Organized leaders are also good managers of time, and they make sure they give team members sufficient time to complete delegated tasks. Organization and time management are essential elements for every high-performing team.

#9 Decency & Order

When it comes to ministry, God does all things decently and orderly. From Genesis to Revelation, He has orchestrated all time, space, and history toward its appointed end. The Lord took ahold of the chaos, darkness, and formless void and subjected it to His divinely designed world, including all of the laws of science, reasoning, and gravity that brought order to chaos. His organizational beauty appears all the more manifest when we observe the intricate detail that went into constructing the temple and all of its accompanying articles, including the Ark of the Covenant. Undoubtedly, the God we serve is precise, organized, and acts with deliberate intentionality and purpose. We, too, should aspire to do the same.

God has mandated that *"whatever you do, work at it with all your heart, as working for the Lord"* (Colossians 3:23 NIV). We should approach our efforts, labor, and service with a spirit of excellence because we recognize that the Lord is the ultimate beneficiary of all of our efforts. Toward this end, we should not quickly forget that *"from everyone who has been given much, much will be demanded"* (Luke 12:48 NIV). These truths alone should inspire better organization in all Children's Ministry contexts. When read collectively, it is clear that we have a great ministry (leading children to Christ), which mandates that we do so with a spirit of excellence and zeal. It requires that we write the vision and make it plain. It requires that we write and record our relevant tasks to prioritize and allocate the precious but finite time properly. It requires our mastery over calendars and established deadlines. It requires that we declutter our space to simultaneously declutter our minds and do the work that God has purposed us to do.

Children's Ministry leaders must develop a long-term view of how they do ministry to maximize every opportunity. God's word reminds us to make the most of every opportunity and to manage our time wisely:

> *"Be very careful, then, how you live-not as unwise but as wise, making the most of every opportunity because the days are evil."*
>
>   – Ephesians 5:15-16 NIV

> *"Teach us to number our days, that we may gain a heart of wisdom."*
>
>   – Psalms 90:12 NIV

These scriptures highlight God's message that the wisest people are the ones who know the seasons. They're the ones who know how to count the cost. They're the ones who, like Him, anticipate the end from the beginning and orchestrate their lives accordingly.

We see this exemplified by the Proverbs 31 woman. A woman who commits herself to make the most of her day. She gets up before the sun rises, and she works tirelessly through the wee hours of the night, executing on all four cylinders. She has mastered her schedule on a level that every leader should aspire to achieve. Organized leaders can only achieve this level of productivity by triaging all of their to-dos along a continuum of importance. Some tasks are critical, yield high returns, or otherwise demand our immediate attention, and these tasks deserve greater attention and effort. Conversely, some duties are less time-sensitive, critical, or yield lower returns, and these will naturally rank lower on the to-do list. The real strength is developing the maturity and discipline to know what task falls in what bucket.

Ultimately, if your office, ministry space, and overall leadership lack organization, then your children, team, and their families may perceive a lack of care. If you don't prepare or organize, then your programs will come off as rushed, poorly planned, or thrown together at the last minute. As ministry leaders, you never want to convey that message, especially to those looking for leadership. However, **organized leaders convey a message of excellence, thoughtfulness, and intentionality.** With the pressures of ministry, there will certainly be times when you have to throw something together with limited preparation or planning, but this should be the exception and not the rule. Ministry teams that continuously find themselves rushing, improvising, or otherwise scrambling should quickly implement these organizational tips.

The absence of organization not only affects the leader but can ruin the experience of your workers. You want to **be thoughtful when executing each task because when you don't, people notice.** When team members have to operate in chaotic environments continuously, then you risk losing them. Think of the parents. Would you feel comfortable dropping your children off in a space that looks like a hurricane hit it or handing them over to leaders who rushed in only moments before you? No family will remain in a church if the Children's Ministry department appears to be an untrustworthy place for their children's spiritual development. When new families visit and their children are shoe-horned into a basement or a balcony with nothing more than broken crayons and haphazard volunteers, trust and believe they are not coming back! Children's Ministry leaders must accept the truth that **actions, not intentions, speak louder than words**, and your organizational skills are a huge part of that.

To be organized as a Children's Ministry leader takes work! Once you have delegated your responsibilities and have made a schedule, then you can manage what you have to do and when you need to do it. Staying organized is not a breeze in Children's Ministry, but it is possible for every leader who is willing to put in the work. It requires that you: (1) work hard in recognizing what needs to get done, (2) work harder when you need to put in more work, and (3) enjoy a clutter-free ministry life while you advance the work of God. Don't forget that clutter-free environments help productivity. **Organized Children's Ministry leaders get to do more with the time they have. They don't waste time on activities or items that don't add value to the church, the department, the kids, or themselves.** Commit to becoming an organized progressive leader and excel in ministry today.

TECH HACKS 101

◇ Consider various applications such as Evernote, Todoist, Dropbox, and more that can help record your to-dos in a fast and organized way.

◇ Consider investing in smart devices to help keep track of your responsibilities. Smart devices such as Amazon Alexa/ Echo, Google Assistant, and Apple HomePod, just to name a few, are great ways to store everyday tasks and reminders you don't want to forget.

◇ Digital technology helps us to work smarter, not harder. Moving forward, learn to use digital technology to enhance how you organize your space, files, kids, agendas, and life.

KEY INSIGHTS

- *Children's Ministry leaders must learn how to organize their personal lives and the ministry departments they steward.*

- *Learning to write things down is one of the most straightforward steps you can take to enhance your ministry.*

- *Organized leaders set and stick to reasonable deadlines, which result in a better understanding of what they do (or don't) have time to accomplish.*

- *Last-minute notices force all of the Children's Ministry workers involved in the department to scramble. The result is a suboptimal performance and less effective programming for children.*

- *Keeping your department organized means keeping things in a proper place. Organized leaders maintain order by storing, labeling, and managing their items properly.*

- *Don't let your Children's Ministry become the dumping ground for everything that well-intentioned people don't want in their homes.*

- *Progressive Children's Ministry leaders know how to purge with a purpose.*

- *Progressive organized leaders don't give into advertising.*

- *Delegation should be informed by in-depth knowledge of the essential roles and responsibilities together with the strengths, weaknesses, and capacity of your team.*

- *Progressive leaders organize their days around their optimal hours.*

- *Organized leaders convey a message of excellence, thoughtfulness, and intentionality.*

- *Be thoughtful when executing each task because when you don't, people notice.*

- *Organized Children's Ministry leaders get to do more with the time they have. They don't waste time on activities or items that don't add value to the church, the department, the kids, or themselves.*

DISCUSSION QUESTIONS

1. Share a time when you forgot a responsibility. Did it undermine your credibility or otherwise cause problems?

2. How has procrastination caused you to miss a deadline or forced you to scramble to accomplish something in your ministry?

3. Do you struggle to review and purge your Children's Ministry area regularly? If so, what aspects of reviewing or purging are so challenging for you? What can you get rid of today to make more space?

4. Which of the organizational tips resonate with you the most? Why?

5. Do you have a methodology by which you prioritize your to-do list? Do those tasks that are deemed most important or otherwise yield the highest return get most of your attention? Why or why not?

6. Can you share an experience where lack of organization may have made a poor impression of you or your ministry?

CHAPTER 5

"To add values to others, one must first value others."
-John Maxwell

PROGRESSIVE LEADERS VALUE PEOPLE

Ministry is about people. Unfortunately, we live in a society where people are often reduced to their gifts, resources, or talents. This is true for the church in many ways. In the church and the world, it is not uncommon for people to be more celebrated or recognized not for their intrinsic value as a people created in God's image but instead for what they bring to the table or can offer the church. It's great to have gifts and talents. We love incredibly gifted people. However, you can be extremely talented as a Children's Ministry director, coordinator, or leader but be terrible with people. Bottomline, you may know the right colors to paint the room. You know how to execute curriculum like a boss. You know how to structure the storage area in your department like no other. You even possess the skills to pull off a dynamic community event, but if you are horrible working with people you are missing the boat big time! Ministry is, and will always be, about people. Progressive leaders need to have an appreciation for people. **Children's Ministry leaders who don't learn to embrace differences and value people will be extremely limited in what they can accomplish.**

Leaders need to value their team members. Leaders need to respect other leaders. While they must never lose sight of the goal, they must recognize it takes people to achieve it. Nothing splendid has ever been accomplished in pure isolation. People matter in ministry. People matter in Children's Ministry. Progressive leaders believe in the people they lead. Do you? Unfortunately, a lot of church leaders will use people but will rarely authentically believe in them. **If we're not careful in the hustle and bustle of ministry, we can find ourselves pushing for service week after week without understanding and appreciating the people providing the service.** Children's Ministry leaders need to *connect* with the people who co-labor alongside them and know them beyond their service to the department. There are far too many Children's Ministry leaders struggling with developing a healthy approach to valuing and trusting their people.

Learning to Trust

Some leaders fail to value others because they simply don't trust anyone. These leaders frequently battle with burnout and overextend themselves doing a majority of the work. Despite being surrounded by people who can support them and legitimately want to serve, these leaders prefer to work alone because they believe no one else can do the job. **Progressive leaders trust and believe in the people they lead.** I learned the importance of trusting your team while leading one of my first community Easter egg events. At the time, the church I was working for did an excellent job engaging the surrounding community. They developed high expectations around Christmas, Fall Festivals, and VBS programming and looked to garner more engagement through a community Easter egg hunt. I, too, was eager to do an excellent job with the hunt. I envisioned a massive egg hunt, in-door Easter puppet extravaganza with various showings, photo booths, an indoor theme park, carnival-like games, and more! In retrospect, my vision exceeded my underdeveloped volunteer base.

While the event was ultimately a success, it wasn't without many late nights and undue weight placed on my family and other church staff. If I could repeat the preparation, there were probably other volunteers that could have fielded the puppet ministry, selected the art for the photo booth, or even shopped for the candy. But for some reason, it didn't dawn on me to ask for help or delegate to others until it was a little too late to do so. I learned early on how easy it is to be overwhelmed when you decide to handle everything yourself.

My Easter egg hunt taught me another valuable lesson about leadership. While we must trust our team, trust has its limits. **Progressive leaders regularly take stock of their teams and entrust critical tasks to trustworthy individuals.** We all know that there is no Easter egg hunt without Easter eggs. Well, you guessed it! In a desperate day-of-the-event scramble, I allowed an eager group of young volunteers to assist me with hiding the Easter eggs. Instead of providing the necessary oversight, I was too busy monitoring three in-door stations to realize that they had only hidden ½ of the eggs. While the first few egg hunts went off without a hitch, the latter egg hunts were closer to a scene from the movie "*The Hunger Games,*" as the kids fought tooth and nail to grab one of those precious few lingering eggs. You can imagine my horror and humiliation when I discovered ½ of the eggs sitting in the backroom. Let's just say there were a lot more "candy prizes" handed out that summer! As leaders, we must continually push ourselves to value and trust our people, but we must do so with wisdom. Don't ask the team member who is notoriously late to open the early service or the one with the unreliable car to coordinate the carpool. God has given us wisdom, and we should use it when entrusting essential tasks to the people on our teams.

Past Issues with Trust

Trust is a foundational building block in all successful Children's Ministries. If you're going to build a powerful ministry, you have to trust and believe in the people you lead. Yet trust doesn't come naturally to all of us. Unfortunately, some people struggle mightily with trust issues, which, if left unchecked, can severely undermine the fruitfulness of their ministries (and personal lives, for that matter). Issues of trust have many root causes. Some people may struggle because of the hurt they may have experienced within the church. Others battle with trust because of personally witnessing past failures of leadership – sacred and secular leaders. Many leaders have matriculated in environments where there was little to no trust. Their parents trusted very few people. The people they lived around trusted and respected very few people. Maybe they went through a traumatic experience that caused them to distrust most people, and now it is affecting the way they lead the department. At the end of the day, if you operate from a place of distrust, then your department will not be able to produce at the level it's supposed to. It will hinder the way you teach and train others because you don't believe they can learn. This same lack of trust only serves to further complicate proper delegation in Children's Ministry. **When leaders don't believe the people around them have the capacity to execute as they do, they limit the impact that their department can bring to the church, families, and community at large.** Please remember, if you're going to be a progressive leader, you have to learn to trust and believe in the people you lead. Here are a few things that you want to make sure you're doing.

1. **Keep the lines of communication open:** Communication feeds genuine connection and trust. You have to keep the lines of communication open when it comes to working with people. You're not a dictator. You're a leader. You want to **share the vision with the team and enable them to be a part of the development process.** Input from others will help your ministry flourish when you understand that you don't know it all.

2. **Get close to your people:** Proximity helps you to keep a pulse on the ministry. It would help if you got close enough

to your team to read your department's pulse by hearing, seeing, and feeling what's going on through interaction. It is impossible to see everything that is happening in your ministry. Very few people systematically report important details of what's going on in the Children's Ministry, church, or community. The pulse, development, mood, and culture of your ministry are much easier to ascertain and understand when you're building healthy relationships with people. **Leaders build healthy departments by being equally committed to building people.**

3. **Show respect:** Progressive leaders show respect to their team members. Respect must be an undercurrent of all interactions between you and your teams within a Children's Ministry environment. Lamentably, when some people get a title, it's accompanied by an unhealthy belief that they're the "boss" and "it's all about them." If you want a progressive Children's Ministry department, you want to learn how to respect your various team members. Everybody can offer valuable insights. You don't want to be known as the "my way or the highway" department. **A Children's Ministry department that functions exclusively off one person's desires will undoubtedly struggle to reach its full potential.** Respect your team members and give them a forum and opportunity to add value to the Children's Ministry department. Their rich views, perspectives, and experiences will only serve to drive a more dynamic ministry.

"It's only lonely at the top when you take the journey by yourself."

People over Programming

A progressive leader is aware and responsive to the needs of their members. They appreciate that many other things are going on in the lives of team members, the children, and the parents. Are you? You can't be so self-absorbed and myopic that you become oblivious to the often chaotic lives of the people you serve. Despite your busy schedule as a Children's Ministry leader, it's not all about vacation bible school. It's not all about the Fall Festival. It's not all about the Christmas program. It's not all about the curriculum. It's not all about the gift shop or the check-in station. It's about the people. People over programming! You have to authentically care about people – volunteers, children, and families. **Progressive Children's Ministry leaders must commit to being aware of where people are and how to connect with them genuinely.** John Maxwell once said, "People don't care about how much you know until they know how much you care." Progressive leaders build Children's Ministry departments where the team is encouraged to daily express the heart of Christ through their genuine, compassion-filled and intimate relationships with one another.

Progressive leaders also show an interest in their people's ministry aspirations. It's essential to stay close to the people who serve in your department so that you can learn how they specifically desire to add value. In Children's Ministry, flexibility is essential. However, **your team will continue to dwindle if you regularly ignore people's ministry preferences and only place them where there is a need.** The whole point is to connect with them and then stay connected. Be intentional and ask questions. How are things going in the check-in-station? How are things going in the gift shop? How are things going with planning? But don't stop there. Those questions need to serve as a springboard to even deeper ones. How are things going with your son's soccer team? How are things going with your daughter's basketball team? How are things going with you at home? In short, make every effort possible to connect.

One example from a church's music ministry truly brought this point into focus. Like many churches, this music ministry had a paid worship director, but the musicians and praise team were composed entirely of volunteers. One such volunteer's feelings and emotional state was brought up as a powerful lesson to the entire staff. This volunteer, who had served faithfully for the past two years, had made a passing comment about the worship director. During a conversation with another worship team member, he confessed his bouts with depression, financial struggles and even raised some troubling questions about God and his own faith. But the most revealing comment involved the worship director and the drummer's belief that the worship director didn't care about him but was only concerned to the extent he was unable to show up for a particular service. The sobering reality of this lesson shook me to my core. **If our teams don't feel a genuine sense of care or concern, our children and families may likewise feel deprived.**

We must learn to connect with both long-term and short-term workers. The reality is that not everyone who serves in your department has a desire to stay in the department long term, and that's okay! Guess what, they still matter! Maybe someone is serving you faithfully today to fill a need but ultimately desires to be a pastor one day. Perhaps they want to be a deacon, elder, or even go into full-time missions. As their leader, you want to help set the stage for their next role. For example, if someone feels called to be a pastor but has never held a mic, then you should be intentional and caring enough to allow them to lead. Helping them learn how to connect with their audience, teach effectively, and create stage presence shows extreme concern for what matters to them. You need to look into the lives of your people and create opportunities for them to grow. Jesus said, come follow me, and I'll make you fishers of men. Many people believe that Jesus exclusively focused on his mission, but upon closer examination, you will find that this call also involved the disciples' own personal growth and development. Like Christ, **Children's Ministry leaders must embrace that their team's growth and development is part of their responsibility.**

Leaders who care about people not only get their needs met, but they make sure their people's needs are taken care of as well. You've got to make sure that you're equally adding value back when you're getting value from the people who serve on your team. In Children's Ministry, we should always endeavor to arrive at a win/win scenario! A progressive Children's Ministry leader understands that no one wants to lose. Lose/win is never an ideal outcome in ministry. If the church wins and the people lose, the people will leave. If the church loses and the people win, the church will close, and you won't have anywhere to worship. The goal is to strive for a mutually rewarding ministry environment. Strive as much as possible to make sure that the people who serve in your department feel valued and not used.

Another vital part of valuing people is caring enough about their well-being to recognize when they need a break. Children's Ministry leaders should never allow someone to overextend themselves just because they struggle to say "no." There are a lot of people who will always say "yes" to you even when they really can't afford to. Even though you may win, they will lose. Their service to you may cost them their marriage, shortchange their children, or even adversely impact their physical or mental health. Progressive leaders take care of people. They understand that people matter. If you take care of your people, they will take care of your ministry. If you love people enough, they will give their time, talents, and treasures to advance the kingdom of God. Conversely, if you just use people, they will come and go. You will find there's a revolving door of people leaving just as fast as they came because you could not make them feel valued.

"There can be no great success without others."

Love Them

The act of valuing your team can be summed in a single word: **love**. Biblical love is the hallmark of all faith communities and the identifying agent that shows the world we belong to him. Christ himself reaffirmed this truth in the book of John:

> *A new command I give you: Love one another. As I have loved you, so you must love one another. By this everyone will know that you are my disciples, if you love one another.* (John 13:34-35 NIV)

Communities of faith should characterize the love of Christ. Christ modeled his love for the lost and the church, but he also modeled a profound love for his ministry partners and co-laborers. We, too, are called to do the same. We must love the children. We must love our parents. And we must love our volunteers. We can't just view them as supports for our ministry to children. We must recognize that we also have a ministry to them!

Those who work alongside us will know our authenticity through our love for them. So much of the Word is dedicated to love in action. This type of love isn't just expressed in words but in deed. In Children's Ministry, we will inevitably meet many people who are gifted, creative, and endowed with extraordinary natural abilities, but – as the Word reminds us – these ministry gifts all come second to the greatest gift, which is love. **You may read the best books, be an incredible organizer, and be vision-driven, but if you lack a genuine love, care, and concern for people, then it's all just a waste of time.** Progressive Children's Ministry leaders must develop a legitimate concern for the well-being of those around them. They must work to create a ministry where both the children and workers benefit. We have to see our ministry partners as more than warm bodies to fill vacancies, but as God's servants entrusted to us for further growth, development, and equipping in ministry.

We must help to cultivate within them a heart that sees Children's Ministry as far more than a babysitting club but rather a powerful ministry that has the power to spark a revival in the hearts of this next generation of boys and girls. Revival fire ignites in a team of people who feel valued and loved.

From a practical standpoint, loving others with genuine affection and concern doesn't happen naturally for many of us. **As leaders, we must ask God to cultivate a heart in us for the people around us.** Over the years, I have encountered countless people who were uncomfortable with children, but they were willing to see past their own comfort zones for the sake of the Ministry. As time progressed, I would watch as God was transforming their hearts for the children they served. A heart that didn't previously exist. One of Children Ministry greats, the late Craig Jutila, shared his own reluctant experience when being called to serve children in his book, Leadership Essentials for Children's Ministry:

> *"Listen, I know all of us found our way into ministry one way or another. Some were called. Some were chosen. I was dragged-listless, apathetic, and downright protesting. But God changed my heart."*
>
> *-Craig Jutila*

Maybe you've had a similar experience. I, too, struggled with the desire to want to do something. This was particularly true for me when it came to serving the homeless. I wanted so badly to jump into serving the *least of these* with the full heart and compassion of Christ. Unfortunately, my first ministry experience didn't quite line up with those expectations. I will never forget being invited by one of my seminary classmates to serve alongside him and his wife at a homeless family shelter. I was ecstatic! I would finally be able to walk in Christ's shoes by serving a community that was indeed in need.

I could hardly contain my excitement as we waited in the classroom until the residents finished dinner. We had already worked out a game plan where I would focus on the children while my friends would be teaching their parents. I thought to myself; this will be one of the most rewarding experiences of my life. How could it not be? I was combining my passion for serving children with my desire to reach the least of these. What could go wrong? Well, a lot went wrong. The kids were everywhere, and I had absolutely no control. What's worse, when the cutest one escaped to the front podium, she whacked me a good one in the face as I attempted to pick her up. Equally embarrassed and mortified, I wanted nothing more than for that evening to end. When my friends invited me back the following week, let's just say I may or may not have been available. No way was I going back there!

But then something happened. I went back, and then I went back again and again. I got to know the kids by name. I would sit and have conversations with them. They would pull up a chair and have conversations with me. They began calling me by name and would wave at me through the glass windows of the shelter when they saw me making my way up the sidewalk to spend time with them. It wasn't long until love for them began to fill my heart. I began to wonder how they were doing and what they were doing. Did Miranda's mom get that job we were praying for, or did Michael's dad get the help he needed so they could finally be a family again? Their concerns became my concerns, and I wanted nothing more than to see them flourish in their lives and faith.

So how are you in the love department? Be willing to acknowledge and accept that this may be an area where you (and all of us) could use a bit more attention. There's no shame in it. We've all been there before. Loving others doesn't always happen overnight, and it may take some time, especially if you've been burned before. But I encourage you to keep praying and sowing into it by placing yourself in uncomfortable situations. God can change your heart and mind as you continue to take advantage of those opportunities that He gives you to love others. **Children's Ministry leaders must look for, and create, opportunities to love on their teams, children, and even difficult parents.** Being intentional about actively loving others will make you an influential minister, an effective leader, and a powerful Christian. Some of the most dynamic ministries are led by leaders who allowed themselves to be moved by compassion. Is your ministry to children and families one that is motivated by compassion? If it's not, it's time to pray and go to work. Even a simple thank you note or phone call to let someone know that you're thinking about them during a difficult time can go a long way.

Demonstrating genuine love, care, and concern for others in your sphere of influence doesn't have to be complicated, complex, or burdensome. Some of the practical ways that I have seen this done in action include:

- Handwritten thank-you notes after someone has done something valuable
- Public recognition for their contributions to the ministry
- Showing up at a sporting event or personal moment that is entirely unrelated to the ministry
- An unsolicited and random phone call to ask them how they are doing
- Going out of your way to find them on Sunday just to let them know how much you appreciate their contributions
- A thoughtful gift upon a return trip from a conference, vacation, or another outing

Every Children's Ministry's goal is to learn to respect the leaders above them, beside them, and beneath them. Make sure that everyone feels valued. Make sure that everyone is getting something out of this. Make sure that when you show up, you're the leader that loves people. You're the leader that helps people. You're the leader who people prize for the deposits you have made to their lives and ministries. As Jesus said to his disciples, you too want to say, come follow me in the Children's Ministry, and I'll help you to become better. Jesus had phenomenal people skills. While most people would have dumped Peter after his public denial, Jesus saw past his failure to help unlock his potential. While most people would have simply attended Lazarus' funeral, Jesus saw life and an opportunity to glorify God even in the most hopeless situations. Progressive leaders care about people and speak life to those who are dying. They connect with those who they call team members. Caring leaders know how to weep with the weeping, mourn with the mourning, and rejoice with the rejoicing. Moving forward, choose to be a progressive leader who understands that people matter.

TECH HACKS 101

◇ Consider using digital technology to send appreciation gifts to members of your team.

◇ Practice sending appreciation text messages. Don't be lazy! Make this personal to the individual. 60% of people agree that personalized messages mean a lot more than group texts.

◇ Create videos to celebrate your team members. The videos could include the outstanding work of someone on your team, birthday messages, job promotions, personal triumphs, and more. Bottom line, find ways to use digital technology to brag on your team and make them feel like a hundred bucks!

KEY INSIGHTS

- *Children's Ministry leaders who don't learn to embrace differences and value people will be extremely limited in what they can accomplish.*

- *In the hustle and bustle of ministry, if we're not careful, we can find ourselves pushing for service week after week without understanding and appreciating the people providing the service.*

- *Progressive leaders trust and believe in the people they lead.*

- *Progressive leaders regularly take stock of their teams and entrust critical tasks to trustworthy individuals*

- *When leaders don't believe the people around them can execute as they do, they limit their department's impact on the church, families, and community.*

- *Leaders build healthy departments by being equally committed to building people.*

- *A Children's Ministry department that functions exclusively off one person's desires will undoubtedly struggle to reach its full potential.*

- *your team will continue to dwindle if you regularly ignore people's ministry preferences and only place them where there is a need.*

- *If our teams don't feel a genuine sense of care or concern, then our children and families may likewise feel deprived.*

- *Children's Ministry leaders must embrace that their team's growth and development is part of their responsibility.*

- *Another vital part of valuing people is caring enough about their well-being to recognize when they need a break.*

- *As leaders, we must ask God to cultivate a heart in us for the people around us.*

- *Children's Ministry leaders must look for, and create, opportunities to love on their teams, children, and even difficult parents.*

DISCUSSION QUESTIONS

1. Where are you on the trust spectrum? Do you generally trust your team, or would you say that there is still some level of distrust? Explain.

2. What events in your life have served to increase or decrease how quickly you trust people?

3. What are some things you can do to help build trust with your team?

4. What are some of the things that you have done to connect and get closer to your team? If not much, what are some things you can start doing today?

5. How are you effectively keeping the pulse on your Children's Ministry?

6. Have you ever been a part of a ministry where you felt you were continuously on the short end of the (win/lose) stick? If so, what are some ways to make it more of a mutually rewarding (win/win) experience for your team?

7. What are some ways to practically demonstrate love or genuine concern to your children, parents, and Children's Ministry workers?

CHAPTER 6

"Above all else, guard your heart, for everything you do flows from it."
Proverbs 4:23 (NIV)

PROGRESSIVE LEADERS ARE
NOT EASILY OFFENDED

While leaders are ever focused on serving families and presenting the gospel to children, they must also appreciate that they will inevitably do something that will offend someone. God doesn't exempt ministers from trouble, trials, or challenges simply because we're in ministry. In fact, he guarantees we will have our fair share of it! When it comes to offense, God wants us to position ourselves to where we don't allow ourselves to become angry, bitter, or resentful. I have met quite a few Children's Ministry leaders who, to this day, remain mad or hurt because of how someone treated them in the ministry. **It is vital that Children's Ministry leaders not allow a person or a situation to make them so angry that it affects how they serve.** In this chapter, I would like to examine how Children's Ministry leaders protect themselves from a spirit of offense. Progressive leaders operate beyond wrongs and shield themselves from falling victim to its devastating consequences.

Offenses are Inevitable

As a starting point, we need to acknowledge that awful situations are bound to occur. It's not bad to experience offense unless we allow it to contaminate us or our ministries. Offenses are a part of living in an imperfect world with imperfect people. Whether we like it or not, an offense will come. Just as much as we should be slow to take offense, we should equally be aware of the ways we can unknowingly offend others. With rampant insecurities and unhealthy emotions, people will find reasons to be offended. Some people come into your environment who still carry offenses from their last church or ministry area. Even though they may have a genuine heart to serve in the Children's Ministry department, these leaders' hearts are damaged, which may cause you to become the target of their pain.

You'd be surprised to discover that even individuals who get promoted to leadership positions are susceptible to holding on to residual grudges. Hurt feelings linger because they never address the offense. The problem or hurt grew into a root of bitterness. Then hurt begins to color all of their encounters and leads to even greater offenses. When people harbor hurt and animosity, the ramifications can devastate the children, families, and department.

I will never forget meeting a worker I had inherited in our Children's Ministry department. When I came on board I immediately recognized her as an incredible volunteer in our Children's Ministry. When it came to being faithful, I can't tell you how much joy and relief she brought to my heart as a leader. She would show up early and leave late. I could literally oversleep and wouldn't miss a beat. When I would arrive at the church, the lights would be on, she would unlock the doors, and the Children's Ministry would be 100% ready to go without me lifting a finger! But that was who she was. She was a leader for large events, a Sunday school teacher, a children's church worker, a Children's Ministry Council member, and everything else in between. When it came to reliability, She took home the gold prize week after week. However, when it came to grudges, let's just say that she earned herself some demerits. Her unwillingness to work with particular people because of the spirit of offense was a pain in this leader's rear end. I just couldn't wrap my mind around how someone could be so incredibly faithful to the Children's Ministry on the one hand and yet so immature on the other. She began to aggressively take on roles, including ones she was ill-suited to perform, because of her outright refusal to work with certain people. She was so mired in past hurt that she would even threaten to leave the Children's Ministry from time to time if we invited particular people to serve alongside her. Unfortunately, all of her ultimatums resulted in a much-needed reality check and crucial confrontation that none of us wanted. Her grudges didn't just hurt her. They hurt the children, families, and ultimately the Children's Ministry department.

As leaders, we must learn to recognize the destructive power of offense. Satan tries to use the spirit of offense to destroy lives. Ultimately, offense is inevitable. But the question is, how will you respond when it comes? Will you be pure in spirit grounded by a healthy relationship with God so that you remain undefiled by any bitterness? Ultimately, if you ask God to extend grace towards you for your shortcomings, you must likewise extend grace and forgiveness towards those who fail you. Scripture emphasizes the importance of promptly extending forgiveness so that you do not become a slave to anger and bitterness:

> *In your anger do not sin. Do not let the sun go down while you are still angry, and do not give the devil a foothold.*
> – Ephesians 4:26 (NIV)

The Bible tells us the position we must take as believers. As noted above, there will always be situations that anger or offend us, but Scripture counsels us not to linger, dwell, or even go to sleep when angry. The results of harboring animosity can be debilitating. A 2012 study published in the *Journal of Behavioral Medicine* discovered that when people were only willing to forgive others under certain conditions-like the other person apologized or promised to never repeat the same behavior–their risk of dying early actually increased. Ultimately, you don't have control over whether someone will apologize. Waiting to forgive people until they say they're sorry gives them control over not just your life, but perhaps even your death. It will always be Satan's goal to cause division between friends, church leaders, and congregations. You could have a great vision for your Children's Ministry department, but the enemy can completely throttle your success through seeds of discord and offense. Don't give him that power! Offenses have the potential to damage, destroy, and kill a Children's Ministry department. But practicing forgiveness is the best way to keep the enemy from luring you into a situation that will hinder you, your communion with God, and relationships with other people. **For progressive leaders, forgiveness is an essential practice for navigating the inevitable offenses that ministry brings without sacrificing the forward progress or people that bring it to fruition.**

"The offense you hold today will sabotage your success tomorrow."

Developing a Biblical Response to Offense

As leaders, we must invite God to work within our hearts to develop a Biblical response to offense. This is imperative for Children's Ministry leaders. We need to allow God to come in and do his necessary work in our hearts to ensure that we don't go into ministry polluted by negative or critical thoughts or attitudes toward others. We have to invite Him in daily. God has the power to use past or current offenses to develop our character and spiritual maturity. A natural response to an offense is to pull back and set up an emotional wall to avoid future hurts. If you allow Christ to harness offense for your spiritual growth and development, you must put your ego aside. As a Children's Ministry Leader, you must ask yourself these questions:

- Do I have to be, right?
- Do I have to get my way?
- Can I set aside my feelings and consider the best interest of others?
- Is my response to this offense reflective of a desire to see Christ glorified?

By honestly answering these questions from a Biblical standpoint, you will be positioning your Children's Ministry to thrive. The book of Proverbs reminds us of this truth:

> *A person's wisdom yields patience; it is to one's glory to overlook an offense.*
>   – Proverbs 19:11 (NIV)

Sometimes, as leaders, you must *choose* to overlook someone's behavior to avoid strife and any corresponding disturbance in your spirit. Failure to do so may result in unhealthy disputes, drama, and conflicts that have the potential to malign your credibility, tarnish your relationships, and disrupt the effectiveness of your ministry. Some people will offend you unintentionally, while the devil is merely using others. Leaders must recognize the tactics of the enemy and move beyond them. We must always remember that we don't war against flesh and blood but have an adversary that is hell-bent on destroying anything and everything associated with Christ and the advancement of his kingdom. Ultimately, God calls leaders to be mature and to respond appropriately. That's why they're leaders. They are uniquely called and equipped for such a time as this. **Leaders must not be tossed to and fro by petty disputes but must recognize that their heavenly assignment will carry with it some battle scars.** They must realize that they will encounter some situations that call for Christ-like restraint. Even though they may be falsely accused or have their reputations crucified, they – like Christ – must rise above and patiently endure for the sake of God's ultimate plans and purpose.

Progressive leaders are selective in when and how they respond to offenses. You cannot respond to everything that happens to you or everything that happens around you. The progressive leader must prioritize the work that they are doing for God over personal slights or irritations. If you are quick to respond to every little offense, you will be one frustrated leader. Progressive leaders understand **God getting His glory should always supersede our feelings.** The choice is up to you. You can choose who will win. When encountering an offense, it is natural only to perceive things from your perspective. But offenses take on a completely different aspect when we realize that they are very often spiritual dimensions to the conflicts we face, particularly for those of us in full-time ministry:

> *For our struggle is not against flesh and blood, but against the rulers, against the authorities, against the powers of this dark world, and against the spiritual forces of evil in the heavenly realm.*
>
> – Ephesians 6:12 (NIV)

For this reason, **God's Word must be ever before us and direct how we view and respond to offenses.** The enemy comes to steal, kill, and destroy! He desires your Children's Ministry department to diminish, struggle, and utterly fail to fulfill its mission in your church and surrounding community. If you are a leader who is drowning in offense, it will ultimately hinder your ministry. Despite the emotional toll that these offenses take, you are never powerless. You have the mind of Christ, the Spirit of God, supernatural weapons, and the indwelling presence of the Father that makes you more than a conqueror through Christ Jesus. As a leader, spiritual and character development should always be a goal for you and your team. We should likewise aspire to help others walk in the spirit of unity instead of offense. Allow someone to get the opportunity to grow. Allow someone to experience a better way. Allow someone to see an exceptional example. BE THE EXAMPLE! Leaders moving forward must be slow to take offense. The Bible says it this way:

> *"My dear brothers and sisters, take note of this: Everyone should be quick to listen, slow to speak, and slow to become angry. Because human anger does not produce the righteousness that God desires."*
>
> — James 1:19-20 (NIV)

Preserving the Peace

Leaders frequently deal with competing interests and viewpoints but must endeavor to preserve harmony and live in peace. Sound counsel is critical in light of humanity's natural tendency to find reasons for division and a demonic foe that seeks to exploit those differences by sowing seeds of discord and watering roots of bitterness among God's people. Bottom line, if you're in ministry, you will experience drama. But progressive leaders can overcome drama by creating common ground. **They refine and avoid all extraneous**

disputes by refocusing people on God's overall mission. In other words, they don't major on the minors. By elevating God's interest above all others, they safeguard themselves and their ministries from falling into needless offense, division, and discord. I love how Christ masterfully modeled this practice. Jesus had plenty of opportunities to be offended, including an incident where he – the Savior of the world – was accused of being a demon. Despite the constant stream of offending triggers, Christ never descended into anger, animosity, or unforgiveness. And the relatively rare instances that did provoke a stronger reaction were done in defense of God's honor (as opposed to his own):

> *Jesus entered the temple courts and drove out all who were buying and selling there. He overturned the tables of the money-changers and the benches of those selling doves. "It is written," he said to them, "My house will be called a house of prayer, but you are making it a den of robbers."*
> – Matthew 21:12-13 (NIV)

Leaders can learn a lot from how Jesus chose to respond to offenses. It was only when God's honor was threatened or disrespected that Jesus took action. **Progressive leaders reserve their energy for the right moments. They refuse to respond with baseless irritation or petty anger but instead react with righteous indignation.** This type of reaction does not happen by simple slights like "you stepped on my toe" or "you stole my credit." Instead, this type of anger and reaction is rooted and grounded in an appropriate response to Biblical or moral injustices. It's not focused on someone feeling slighted, but rather is in response to actions or scenarios that break the heart of God.

Progressive leaders are peacemakers and bridge builders. They anticipate and are on guard against those things that commonly cause strife in the body of Christ. Bitterness can occur when someone doesn't feel honored. Division happens when someone doesn't feel like their voice is being heard. An offense takes place when someone feels like you're stepping into their territory. Not only are they slow to take offense when such issues arise, but progressive leaders strategically neutralize these incidents so that others won't get unduly hurt in the process. They have mastered the Biblical art of using soft words to turn away wrath and using their tongues as instruments of life instead of death.

As a Children's Ministry veteran, I have witnessed more than a few situations where well-meaning Christians allowed their emotions to boil over into some fairly contentious arguments. One such fight erupted over the selection and distribution of – believe it or not – Bibles. Yes, I said it, Bibles. This battle started when an excited church member wanted to purchase several copies of *The Action Bible* and make them available in the church pews for students. If you aren't familiar with this particular translation of the Bible, it is stylized like a comic book to appeal to a younger generation. The Children's Pastor wasn't sold on the idea of adding the bibles to their more traditional Bibles that were typically available and initially shot down the idea. In their zeal, the church member decided to approach the senior pastor with the idea and fully expected to be lauded for their foresight and financial contribution by the Children's Pastor. Instead, they were met with disappointment and frustration because they had consulted senior leadership after not getting a favorable response to their initial request. While there is absolutely room for debate on the issue of what Bible is the most appropriate for students, this conversation and subsequent encounters devolved into something a lot more vile. By the end of the ordeal, both parties had gotten quite agitated and made personal attacks on one another's character, integrity, and motivations. In hindsight, this situation could have been better handled with grace and humility. For the leader's part, they were offended that someone would be so brazen as to go higher up to get approval for something they had already expressed their disapproval too. Even though there was genuine merit to the proposal, it was even more detestable because the offense consumed the leader. It didn't help that this particular leader struggled with anxiety and countless insecurities. These insecurities were only exacerbated when this church member, in their view, had overstepped into their lane and responsibilities. Talk about the perfect recipe for offenses to multiply and feelings to be hurt. **As leaders, we have got to learn how to check our offenses at the door. Otherwise, we may unintentionally be the cause of our own ruin as volunteers, parents, and co-laborers become victims of our own insecurities.** If you find yourself struggling with a legacy or historical offense, recognize that it's part of the enemy's attack.

"It is sad to see someone who's accomplished so much yet has no joy because they harbor offense."

Christian Confrontation

Offenses are inevitable, but how we respond makes all the difference. If you are in the unenviable position of having been the instigator or victim of an offensive situation, then you too have some work to do. The book of Matthew provides a roadmap of how Believers are to respond to offense:

> *If your brother or sister sins, go and point out their fault just between the two of you. If they listen to you, you have won them over. But if they will not listen, take one or two others along, so that every matter may be established by the testimony of two or three witnesses.*
>
> –Matthew 15-16 (NIV)

The unfortunate truth is, a lot of leaders struggle with this passage because they struggle with confrontation. For many of us, just the word confrontation creates a lump in our throats. However, progressive leaders need to develop the skills to deal with conflict in healthy ways. **Confrontation does not give leaders a license to attack the person who offended them but should be motivated by a spirit of humility, truth, and love.**

These conversations, albeit uncomfortable, can be genuinely transformative if done correctly. Here are a few considerations for healthy confrontation:

- **Be prayerful**. We should always seek God before confronting someone else. You may discover that you are grasping at the speck in someone else's eye and ignoring your own colossal log. Pray that God reveals any way that you may have contributed to the offense. Additionally, pray for God's wisdom, humility, and compassion as you approach the conversation.
- **Own your Actions**. Be sober-minded about your own role in the offense. Even if you weren't the aggressor, if your

reaction wasn't ideal, be prepared to acknowledge your own shortcomings in the encounter.

- **Timing is everything**. These can be emotionally-charged conversations. You should be thoughtful as to the time, place, and temperament of the other person. Ideally, you will select a time and venue that isn't prone to distraction, disruption, or other logistical complications. Similarly, you want to be sure that the other person is in a healthy emotional state to have the conversation.

- **Be forward-looking**. While you need to address the wrong, you should focus on shared goals, areas of common ground, and hopes for the relationship's future. If you desire to experience an improved working relationship, healthier ministry, or better communication, then root your conversation in that future state. Progressive leaders have a vision, and that vision should motivate both parties to want to move beyond the current offense.

- **Be led by love**. Above all, allow the interaction to exemplify the love of Christ. If he was able to overlook the offense of the cross for the sake of love, we too could overcome any offense for the sake of his kingdom. Let Jesus be your model for effective confrontation.

So how do you respond to an offense? Are you approaching the conversation with a real heart for reconciliation, or is it just a forum to get your grievance addressed? Do you allow your offenses to fester, or do they bleed into other relationships or even impact your worship? As ministers of reconciliation, what better example of God's forgiveness than His servants' ability to pursue forgiveness and reconciliation in their personal lives? God wants us to prioritize reconciliation because He knows the havoc of unforgiveness. **No past hurt is worth disruptions to our prayer lives, bitterness in our relationships, or the spiritual death or stagnation of our churches and the departments we lead.**

It's important to know that the way we choose to handle offense not only affects us but those who respect us as leaders. **Handling offenses poorly can jeopardize our reputation and cause those around us to question our character.** Every good work, life changed, and powerful ministry event will instantaneously evaporate after just one poorly handled offense. Michelle was a dedicated leader to the children and families. Yet through one act of offense, she got infected and then spread it across the whole church. What started as a seemingly minor conflict grew into an angry faction that culminated in 15 people leaving the church. The root cause was a single offense. Devastation happens when leaders fall victim to an offense. We are all human. We are bound to hurt one another occasionally, but we must always cling to this fundamental truth that should ultimately override any offense:

> *Above all, love each other deeply, because love covers over a multitude of sins.*
>
> — 1 Peter 4:8 (NIV)

Leaders must epitomize this truth, even when confronted with great offense. If handled well, offenses can create opportunities to really solidify and strengthen relationships. Despite the discomfort, I've had moments when I had to confront someone to reveal that their actions or words hurt me. But God used those vulnerable conversations, motivated by love, to heal emotional wounds and motivate deeper respect and appreciation for all the parties involved. Only by addressing hurts head-on will you be able to enjoy healthy relationships.

TECH HACKS 101

◊ Digital forms of communication tend to lack feeling and proper expression, which may lead to negative interpretation. As a leader, make sure you're not over reading texts, emails, etc. Remember, Progressive Children's Ministry leaders are not easily offended.

◊ Conversely, when dealing with an offense, it's always better to meet in person or just pick up a phone. If this is not possible, consider using digital platforms that invite proper expression and allows both parties to see one another like Facetime, Marco Polo, or Zoom.

KEY INSIGHTS

- *It is vital that Children's Ministry leaders not allow a person or a situation to make them so angry that it affects how they serve.*

- *For progressive leaders, forgiveness is an essential practice for navigating the inevitable offenses that ministry brings without sacrificing the forward progress or people that bring it to fruition.*

- *As leaders, sometimes you must choose to overlook someone's behavior to avoid strife and any corresponding disturbance in your spirit.*

- *Leaders must not be tossed to and fro by petty disputes but must recognize that their divine appointment will carry with it some battle scars.*

- *God getting His glory should always supersede our feelings.*

- *God's Word must be ever before us and direct how we view and respond to offenses.*

- *Progressive Leaders refine and avoid all extraneous disputes by refocusing people on God's overall mission.*

- *Progressive leaders reserve their energy for the right moments. They refuse to respond with baseless irritation or petty anger but instead respond by righteous indignation.*

- *As leaders, we have got to learn how to check our offenses at the door. Otherwise, we may unintentionally be the cause of our own ruin as volunteers, parents, and co-laborers become victims of our own insecurities.*

-   *Confrontation does not give leaders a license to attack the person who offended them but should be motivated by a spirit of humility, truth, and love.*

-   *No past hurt is worth disruptions to our prayer lives, bitterness in our relationships, or the spiritual death or stagnation of our churches and the departments we lead.*

DISCUSSION QUESTIONS

1. Have you ever been so offended in the context of ministry that you have tempted to harbor a grudge against someone?

2. Do you view your offenses as an opportunity to glorify God?

3. How can you use the overall vision and common ground to avoid conflict and preserve peace in your Children's Ministry?

4. Are you selective about the offenses that occupy your attention? When is it appropriate to express righteous indignation?

5. How does Jesus' response to conflict and offense motivate you?

6. What are some practical ways you can handle offensive situations in your ministry?

CHAPTER 7

*"Trust in the Lord with all thine heart; and lean
not unto thine own understanding. In all your ways
acknowledge him, and he shall direct thy paths."*
-Proverbs 3:5-6 (NIV)

PROGRESSIVE LEADERS ARE SPIRIT-SENSITIVE

We serve the Lord Jesus Christ. In the words of the Apostle Paul, *"in him we live, and move, and have our being"* (Act 17:27), and our ministries will only reach their fullest potential if and when they are submitted and remain wholly devoted to Christ. God's spirit must always play the lead role within our ministries if we truly desire to reach children and families. Even if you're an avid reader, team-oriented, and vision-driven, if the Lord doesn't build your ministry, then you are still laboring in vain. While all of the previous chapters serve as excellent advice and counsel, **Children's Ministry leaders must be careful not to get so caught up in practical methods or best practices that they lose sensitivity to God's purposes.** Above all, God is in control, and even the best-laid plans may have to take a back seat to what the Lord is leading us to do. There is a great temptation among leaders to be overly dependent on our natural intellect, work ethic, and creativity. Yet God's word reminds us that it's *"not by might nor by power, but by my Spirit says the Lord Almighty"* (Zechariah 4:6) (NIV). Stated differently, leaning on God's Spirit supersedes any form of self-reliance. As believers, we have the mind of Christ, and we would be foolish to neglect it. It is precisely this divine support that undergirds Christ's statement that his followers would advance to do *"even greater works"* than he. What an incredible gift! **The Holy Spirit takes what we can do in our natural strength and supernaturally empowers our efforts!**

So, let me ask you a question. Do you believe that God is going to speak to you and through you? Everything that we do in our ministries must be under the authority of Christ. We must lead with the mindset that our ministries belong to him, and he trusts us with a sacred responsibility and mandate. Leaders cannot just take the ball and run with it apart from him. He is the potter, and we are the clay. He should be shaping our ministries. He should be directing all of the initiatives, programming, and efforts of our ministries. Everything that we do is for Christ, with Christ in mind, and with the overall objective, Christ will speak through us. Our aim is not to outdo other ministries, obtain accolades, or secure the praise or approval of people, but so that we-- like John the Baptist – may decrease so that Christ may increase all the more. Plain and simple, **you can't do ministry without the Spirit of God.** If you do ministry in your own strength, you invite an exhausting, stressful, and self-reliant ministry motivated by carnality and self-sufficiency. A Children's Ministry department that is self-sufficient will not stand. Sensitivity to the Holy Spirit is a nonnegotiable must for all ministry leaders, particularly for those called to serve the youngest of the flock. Leaders who are not interested in being Spirit-led should not be leading in ministry.

Scripturally Grounded

So, what does it mean to be a Spirit-sensitive leader? Number one, it means that we have to be grounded in Scripture. The Bible has to be the prevailing justification behind what we do and why we do it. **Progressive Leaders do not treat the Bible as antiquated**

words on a page, but they *cherish* it as the life-giving words of God. They know that His Word goes forth and does not return void. They understand that the world was framed by it, and it will not pass away, diminish in its potency, or ever fail. They have personally experienced its goodness in their own lives and intimately know its power to save, heal, and deliver. As ministers of the Gospel, Progressive leaders understand that Christ is the Word made flesh, and, therefore, Scripture holds an unassailable position as the centerpiece of their lives and ministries. They are the living epistles that have dedicated themselves to teaching, training, and living out these precepts' timeless truth to children. Pray that our Heavenly Father blesses you and your co-laborers with an uncommon love for His Word. If we want sustained spiritual success, then we must all endeavor to heed the admonition of the Apostle Paul to his young protégé when sharing timeless wisdom for all ministry leaders:

> *Do your best to present yourself to God as one approved, a worker who does not need to be ashamed and who correctly handles the word of truth.*
>
>   - 2 Timothy 2:14 (NIV)

Now, we can never allow our consumption of Scripture to convert us into modern-day Pharisees and Sadducees. An unfortunately high number of men and women in full-time ministry fall victim to "Sadducee Syndrome," where they are so consumed with the programmatic, external, or behavioral elements of ministry that they completely miss the move of the holy spirit. Are the kids quiet? Are they listening? Are their butts in the seat? Did the game-time run smoothly? Did praise and worship go off without a hitch? Are leaders where they're supposed to be? Yes, all of these things are important, but if we become too focused on these matters, then we risk sacrificing real transformative ministry for the sake of pomp and circumstance. Stated scripturally, we never want our Children's Ministry described as having *"a form of godliness but denying its power"* 2 Timothy 3:5 (NIV).

Ministries led by such leaders struggle to keep families because they have no spiritual substance or weight to them. In short, leaders cannot get so focused on the programming that they miss the heart of God. Implementation is a constant temptation for many ministry leaders because they want to execute well. Unfortunately, their need for pristine execution can cause them to make the same mistake as Martha and miss the blessing of Mary. Again, the goal of a Children's Ministry leader is to invite children to sit at the feet of Jesus. You can't do that without clothing yourself in the truth of God's Word. Leaders can't allow themselves to be so rushed by their programming, agendas, or great crafts that they leave next to no space for God. Remember, one waters and another plants, but ultimately, we have to trust that God gives the increase.

Cultivating an authentic love of Scripture begins by making daily Bible reading part of your lifestyle. The Bible says it this way:

> *Keep this Book of the Law always on your lips; meditate on it day and night, so that you may be careful to do everything written in it. Then you will be prosperous and successful.*
>
> -Joshua 1:8 (NIV)

Bottom line, there is a distinct anointing that comes on a leader who trusts in God's Word. If you desire to be successful in ministry, fall in love with the Word of God, and commit to knowing it. Children's Ministry leaders should never be ashamed of committing themselves to a deeper understanding of God and His Word. It is possible for you to love children and be ignorant of the Word of God. **You could be committed to serving children, but if you don't commit to loving the God who has called you to serve the children, then your ministry will be self-sufficient and not God-dependent.** Trust me. In these situations, everyone loses. Knowing, embracing, and living God's Word is a foundational element for all spirit-led leaders.

The importance of the Bible in the life of all Christians cannot be understated. *"Thy word have I hid in mine heart, that I might not sin against thee.*" Psalm 119:11 (KJV). His Word must always be our mirror and measuring rod. It is living, active, and judges the motivations and intents of the heart. It is the megaphone that amplifies the voice and will of God. He will never contradict the Bible, so it is of dire importance that leaders commit to learning and living it. Our belief in the truth of the Word must far exceed an academic, psychological, or intellectual pursuit but must go to our very cores and transform the way we live. Our belief must manifest itself in concrete action. The parable of the two builders in Matthew 7 powerfully illustrates this point. Both builders had constructed dwellings. Both builders had their homes battered by torrential winds, heavy rains, and rising streams. Yet only the wise builder's house was able to withstand because *"everyone who hears these words of mine **and puts them into practice** is like the wise man who built his house on the rock."* Matthew 7:24 (NIV, emphasis added). We can't just hear the Word but must activate its power through a zealous application.

Authentic love for God's Word doesn't just affect you but has incredible implications for the children you lead. Picture it. It's the tale of two Children's Ministry leaders. The first, let's call her Dorothy, has a genuine devotional life, regularly studies the Scriptures, and has committed herself to live them out daily. Then there is Rose. She sporadically studies the Scriptures independently but generally considers her lesson preparation as sufficient study time. Apart from Sunday services, Rose's commitment to living out her faith through Biblical application is scant. Which of these two leaders do you think will have a more profound impact on the children? If you have spent any time in Children Ministry, you know that the kids are quite good at sniffing out imposters. In particular, this generation is always looking for genuine articles and authentic ambassadors of faith. Unfortunately, the Roses of the world are just ill-suited to this generation because they will undoubtedly question her faith's sincerity as soon as they detect it is only for show or ritual. Yet the Dorothys of the world presents a very different and welcome change for children. She isn't limited to the scripted curriculum but can pull from personal experience. She doesn't just recite the memory verse, but all of her words – scripted and spirit-led – are in harmony with the will of the Heavenly Father. In short, her ministry is more powerful because it comes out of a deep and abiding personal relationship and love of the Word.

God's desire is for us to become vessels of honor *"useful to the Master and prepared to do any good work."* (2 Timothy 2:20, NIV). This honor is for those who are willing to purify their hearts and transform their minds by the power of God's Word. How do I understand God's standards unless I read them? More importantly, how do I communicate to children week after week the importance of knowing Christ when I don't know him myself? These are all questions leaders must ask themselves. One of the scariest things about ministry is that many people end up going through the motions. They've grown up in the church. They've learned the vernacular, but their lives don't necessarily reflect a growing relationship with Christ. **Leaders should regularly take a step back and soberly evaluate their walk with the Lord.** Don't become a victim of religion. As leaders, we are to teach relationship, not religion. Our faith is more than just following a system of rules and regulations to guarantee us a spot in heaven, but it's about truly knowing the one who died for us, who transforms us and is calling us to live for him.

"Your personal life and your ministry life are inextricably intertwined. Who you are directly impacts what you do in ministry."

Personal Relationship

Progressive Leaders make their personal relationship with God a priority. Like Rose, you are in trouble if your devotion time is exclusively limited to preparation for your weekly programming. Your time with God needs to be treasured as a precious gift. Within their secret places with the Father, progressive leaders train their spiritual ears to be sensitive to God's heart and desires. It is here where they learn the invaluable discipline of being in constant communication with the Father. It is here where prayer becomes synonymous with breathing in the life of the thriving believer. Even when examining David's psalms, the man after God's own heart, it is abundantly clear that such hearts are only forged in the crucible of authentic and abiding relationship. Daniel, the man greatly beloved of God, not only serves as a compelling reminder of the challenges of leadership, but also the spiritual fortitude, godly counsel, and supernatural insight that comes from a strong bond with our Heavenly Father. Even the Apostle Paul's prayer life, captured in many of the epistles, reflects a mature perspective deeply rooted and overflowing from his knowledge, trust, and absolute dependence on God. Like David, Daniel, and Paul, it was their intentionality, tenacity, and God-dependency that catapulted them into their purpose and ministry. If you want to be a Children's Ministry powerhouse for God, then your cup has to be continuously filled by Him. The most effective ministers are those that serve out of the overflow of their personal relationship with God. No matter what our tenure in Children's Ministry, we should all devote ourselves to trusting Him, walking with Him, and learning what pleases Him.

Prayer is the primary vehicle for this connectivity with God. Progressive leaders schedule time daily to commune with God. Simply put, no prayer, no power. **If we want God to show up in our ministries in unimaginable ways, we must connect with Him daily through a healthy prayer life.** The higher the position, the greater the dependency on God. How can you expect to introduce God to children if you don't know Him for yourself? If you're trying to encourage kids to talk to God, you must be talking to God as well. A vibrant connection with God, not a lofty title or position, breeds sound decision making and spiritual development in ministry. A strong relationship with God should always be more prized than holding a leadership position within the church. Leaders who fail to maintain a healthy prayer life are easy targets for a distorted worldview, personal failure, and unfulfilled vision.

A strong relationship with God protects us from the schemes and attacks of the enemy. Never underestimate our enemy. The Bible makes it clear that he came to kill, steal, and destroy and prowls around like a roaring lion seeking whom he can devour. In the absence of a healthy prayer life and commitment to apply the Word, we make ourselves easy targets for the enemy. Leaders should pray for themselves and those within their sphere of influence. Leaders should likewise pray for those who are in leadership over them. Leaders should pray against all forms of danger or attack, seen and unseen. Challenges, trials, and hardships are part of the human condition. Crisis and attacks are part of any ministry, but Progressive leaders seek divine involvement during these incidents. When these challenges emerge in your church, you want prayer to be your first response and driving force. Leaders should likewise pray that God would enhance their discernment. There are predators, abusive guardians, and corrupting influences that desire to harm our children. Parents depend on us to act as watchmen warning them of any schemes or threats to their family. We have an enemy that is formidable and trying to go after our children's hearts and minds. He is lying to them about their identity. He is lying to them about the pleasures of this world. As leaders, we are to stand against that defeated foe and stand up for righteousness, but you can't do that with the weapons of this world. Failure to depend on the Spirit of God during these perilous times sets us up for failure.

The battles for this generation's hearts and minds have never been fiercer, and there is an overwhelming need for Progressive Leaders that have a real connection with God. **The eternal impact we are called to make demands a rare and uncommon communion**

with the Father. This type of impact requires more than just momentary and sporadic quality time with God. It demands that leaders refrain from operating out of spiritual emptiness and exhaustion. The Word of God anticipates a spiritual maturity that is in a state of perpetual growth. From faith to faith and glory to glory, each passing day – for them – is an opportunity to work in ever-increasing righteousness. Progressive Leaders are those that are planted by the rivers of living water. They are planted in God's presence. They are planted in God's Word. They are planted in their prayer closets. They are planted in a community of believers that will sharpen and refine them. And they bear fruit in both their personal lives and in the ministries that they lead. These are the people that have a unique relationship with the Father that invites growth. They have eyes that see and ears that hear.

How does this type of uncommon communion manifest itself in your Children's Ministry? Uncommon communion realizes that ministry starts well-before any children enter the room because it has been bathing them in prayer all week. It doesn't just fill-out a roster of volunteers but seeks divine direction of who should play what role during the service. It doesn't blindly adhere to a preset schedule but gives the Father room to adjust as He so desires. It doesn't stop with sanitized lessons but addresses the real and contemporary issues our children face. It doesn't treat the children as simply another filled-seat but individually connects with them and is discerning enough to know when "Little Suzie" is struggling and needs a bit more attention. Such confidence, empowerment, and assurance comes when abiding in the Lord.

Putting Christ in Children's Ministry

Our ultimate goal is to have a heart like his heart and to be conformed to his image. Our game plan as leaders should always reflect the image of Christ and serve as his hands and feet. What more effective ministry model can one have than channeling Christ into your very own Children's Ministry? Christ is the standard by which we should measure the effectiveness of our ministries. Everything we do is to be done unto the Lord, following his example. As a leader, one of your greatest strengths, albeit often neglected and overlooked, is the ability to operate in the power of Christ. Many of us fail to tap into this reservoir of strength and rely exclusively on our strength and natural abilities when we weren't created to do so. **In ministry, there is a grave danger of the self-sufficiency trap. The risk of carrying out the work of God with human effort is ever-present.** It is a temptation that goes back to Abraham. We know the story well. A man called to be the "father of many nations" with very little natural hope of conceiving this promised child with his wife. That's when the self-sufficiency began. Time had passed, no promised child had arrived, so he had to take matters into his own hands. He and Sarah rationalized that God must need a "little help" with His plan. One thing led to another, and Abraham has a son, Ishmael, but he doesn't precisely fulfill the promise.

This story of Abraham is later used as a powerful allegory to represent two approaches to inheriting the promises of God:

> *For it is written that Abraham had two sons, one by the slave woman and the other by the free woman. His son by the slave woman was born according to the flesh, but his son by the freewoman was born as the result of a divine promise.*
> – Galatians 4:22-23 (NIV)

Simply put, Isaac (Sarah's son) represents inheriting a divine promise by trusting and relying on God, while Ishmael (Hagar's son) represents the product of trying to fulfill God's promise by self-reliance. Are you trying to fulfill God's promise in your own strength? Or are you one of those branches connected to the vine whereby your fruitfulness is a natural outgrowth of Christ? You simply can't do Children's Ministry in your finite strength.

Effective ministry is contingent upon being connected to the vine. Leaders need to understand this fundamental truth: apart from Christ, they can do nothing, but through him, they can do all things. What a powerful picture of our desperate need to remain connected to Christ. Can you imagine a broken tree branch even growing a single leaf? Then why would you think that your Children's Ministry will flourish if its leaders are operating apart from an abiding relationship with Christ? The whole point is this: don't walk this road alone! Yes, in this book, we have given you tools, best practices, and leadership insights, but if you retain anything, let it be this: **cling to the garment of Christ! Put his yoke on you. Wear the armor that he's given you.**

A lot of Children's Ministries operate much like the Seven Sons of Sceva. They were the sons of a Jewish chief priest who, impressed by Paul's spiritual exploits, sought to mimic his authority to cast out some demons. Unfortunately, their efforts backfired when the demon-possessed man responded, *"Jesus I know, and Paul I know about, but who are you?"* and proceeded to give them such a beating that they ran out of the house naked and bleeding (Acts 19: 15-17). These men learned a vital lesson that day. You can't walk in the authority of a Christ that you don't know. Many of us are also getting beat down by the enemy because our connection with Christ is entirely too frail to withstand attacks. Instead of aimlessly beating at the wind, you should be proclaiming to the enemy that these kids are mine! You should see your ministry for the powerful one it is and understand that you are a soldier in God's army, and with His help, you can fight back against the gates of hell. Progressive leaders stand in the gap as watchmen. The children and families in your ministry are your sheep, and you are the under-shepherd. But the under-shepherd is only as effective as his or her connectivity to the master shepherd.

Christian Encounters

Christ was masterful at dealing with people. We have already examined the importance of teamwork, but having a spirit-centered approach to dealing with people can transform all of your human interactions. Ministry is about bridging the gap between the human and the divine. As Children Ministry leaders, you will encounter people with varying views and opinions, accompanied by occasional conflicts and clashes. Yet Spirit-sensitive leaders don't just view their interactions through the lens of their natural eye. What may seem like a routine interaction with a parent in the natural may give way to a genuinely transformative encounter to those who have trained their spiritual eyes. While your natural mind may take offense at a rude comment or an unruly child, your spiritual eyes may identify a powerful ministry opportunity. Being a spirit-led leader is important because what we do isn't just secular but has supernatural dimensions that only God can bring to light.

This is especially true when dealing with conflicts in ministry. It is important that leaders develop the ability to operate from an empathetic heart. Our hearts give us the ability to feel, connect, and be sensitive. Leaders must deal with the ever-changing dynamics of society, culture, and all that is going on in people's lives. It is vital that they learn to be Christ-like and be empathetic while offering hope and redemption. **A leader who doesn't show empathy is a leader that people won't follow.** We can also see the heart of a leader in how they handle discipline and correction. Do their words and actions reflect the compassion of Christ, who disciplines from a place of love? Or is discipline doled out like a combative drill sergeant motivated more by compliance than compassion? Children and workers need to feel that you're not there to hurt them but correct them in love. Even though correction is a part of the ministry, it can have devastating consequences if it isn't spirit led. But discipline, in accordance with God's design, leads to godly repentance, growth, and development. Leaders must know how to correct in love and encourage others. Spirit-led leaders feel and have empathy. They can move beyond their way to God's way.

Spirit-sensitive leaders possess an uncommon emotional maturity because they recognize that they work for the Lord. They have a Christ-likeness to them that says though they slay me, yet will I trust him. They're able to tackle discouragement, hurt, and disappointment from others and still emulate authentic love for their brothers and sisters in Christ because they know that *"Greater love has no one than this, than to lay down one's life for his friends.* (John 15:13, NIV). They never forget that while they were still sinners, Christ died for them. Spirit-sensitive leaders can stare into the face of venomous and unfounded criticism and say, *"forgive them; for they know not what they do"* because they maintain a heavenly perspective that understands the immaturity of others. So even if they are abused, rejected, or treated as second class citizens, they remain undeterred and leave any vengeance in God's capable hands. They resist all backbiting and immaturity because they are supernaturally empowered to love those around them with the love of the Lord.

Walking by Faith

Spirit-sensitive leaders walk by faith and not by sight. If you have spent any time in ministry, then I'm sure you have endured a challenge or two where you had nothing to cling to but the promises of God. There will undoubtedly be seasons where it seems as if all hope is lost. It is precisely during these times when you have no choice but to put on your Jesus glasses. Only then will you recognize that these seemingly hopeless circumstances are fertile ground for God to do His best work. **It's when you reach the end of your natural strength that you leave room for God's *supernatural* to take hold of the situation.** His faithfulness in this regard is manifest across the whole of Scripture. When Egyptians were barreling down on him, Moses saw the supernatural parting of the waters at the Red Sea's edge. By natural standards, the 10 spies were imminently reasonable for believing that they didn't stand a chance of capturing the Promised Land. But it was the two remaining spies, Joshua and Caleb, that viewed the same circumstances through the lens of faith that unlocked the miraculous. There is no other explanation that would lead a young, ill-equipped shepherd boy to charge a giant warrior except for a supernatural understanding that God would be fighting on his side. Because of his relationship with God, Paul was able to rejoice even when he was sitting in prison with sewage running over his feet. Despite these dire circumstances, he declared that he was seated in heavenly places. Only someone viewing things through spiritual eyes would ever consider something as depressing as a sewage-filled prison as a place of honor!

Progressive leaders must cling to this very same faith. It's faith like this that allows them to look a global pandemic in the face and still believe that God is setting the stage for something incredible. Like Abraham, David, and Moses, these leaders have mastered the art of believing God, even when everyone and everything else would dictate otherwise. As Children's Ministry leaders, we will experience times in our ministry when we have to walk by faith and not by sight if we hope to prevail and thrive. Even if our churches are shrinking, our budgets are evaporating, and our workers flee, God is *still* in control. His strength is made perfect in our weaknesses! Spirit-led leaders thrive because they can say and believe that all things are possible regardless of their circumstances! So how spirit led are you?

TECH HACKS 101

◇ Spirit-led leaders must embrace digital technology and systems available to help them reach children and families at the highest level while simultaneously remaining sensitive to the Holy Spirit's leading.

◇ A Children's Ministry leader who becomes more dependent upon digital technology, systems, analytics, and processes rather than the spirit of God will ultimately find themselves in trouble!

◇ Digital technology can never replace the leading of the Spirit.

KEY INSIGHTS

- *Children's Ministry leaders must be careful not to get so caught up in practical methods or best practices that they lose sensitivity to God's purposes.*

- *The Holy Spirit takes what we can do in our natural strength and supernaturally empowers our efforts!*

- *Progressive Leaders do not treat the Bible as antiquated words on a page, but they cherish it as the life-giving words of God.*

- *You could be committed to serving children, but if you don't commit to loving the God who has called you to serve the children, then your ministry will be self-sufficient and not God-dependent.*

- *Leaders should regularly take a step back and soberly evaluate their own personal walk with the Lord.*

- *If we want God to show up in our ministries in unimaginable ways, then we must connect with Him daily through a healthy prayer life.*

- *The eternal impact that we are to make requires more than just momentary and sporadic quality time with God.*

- *A strong relationship with God protects us from the schemes and attacks of the enemy.*

- *In ministry, there is a grave danger of the self-sufficiency trap.*

- *Effective ministry is contingent upon being connected to the vine.*

- *A leader who doesn't show empathy is a leader that people won't follow.*

DISCUSSION QUESTIONS

1. Would you describe your Children's Ministry as God-dependent or self-sufficient? Why?

2. How can you deepen your devotional life and ensure that you are regularly committing yourself to the study and application of Scripture?

3. In what ways have you prioritized prayer in your life? What differences do you think a stronger connection with God would yield in your Children's Ministry?

4. Describe an encounter when you had to correct or discipline someone in your ministry. Was it motivated by love or compliance?

5. What situations in your ministry are you currently facing where you have no other option but to walk by faith?

CONCLUSION

Our ministries to children should always be advancing, improving, developing, strengthening, maturing, and progressing. Subpar leadership will no longer be acceptable in the church of tomorrow. Our children have matriculated in the digital age. With unprecedented access to information and rapidly developing technology, their views of the church, authority, and God are all shifting. If leaders are to reach the next generation, then they must rise to the occasion and operate with a spirit of excellence. Leaders must make the necessary investments in their personal growth and development in order to harness the most innovative methods to reach children for the glory of God. They must no longer function from service-to-service but must move forward strategically with the future in mind. They recognize that their success will never come unilaterally, but only through optimizing their teams. Leaders must declutter their space so they can declutter their minds and better focus on their mission to children and families. Leaders must value people over programming and guard their hearts from offense at all cost. Ultimately, they know that the success of their ministry is completely predicated on their connection to the heart of God.

I pray this book has blessed you as much as it has blessed me writing it. I would love to hear more about it. Drop me a message at childsheart83@gmail.com and let me know what resonated with you the most. You have been appointed for such a time as this. The church is and should always be a beacon of light. Remember, information received and not applied is useless. Together we can reach children if we do so with a spirit of excellence. It is time to become the progressive leader you were called to be.

WORK CITED

1. Cunningham, Anne E. et al. "What Reading Does for the Mind." *Journal of Direct Instruction*, vol. 1, no. 2, Summer 2001, pp. 137-149.

2. Murphy, Mark. "Neuroscience Explains Why You Need to Write Down Your Goals if You Actually Want to Achieve Them." *Forbes* 15 Apr. 2018, pp. forbes.com/sites/markmurphy/2018/04/15/neuroscience-explains-why-you-need-to-write-down-your-goals-if-you-actually-want-to-achieve-them/?sh=514aef907905. Accessed 12 January 2021.

3. Halvorson, Heidi Grant-. *9 Things Successful People Do Differently.* Harvard Business Review Press, 2018.

4. Hunt, V., Layton, D., & Prince, S. "Why Diversity Matters," *McKinsey & Company*, 1 Jan. 2015, https://www.mckinsey.com/business-functions/organization/our-insights/why-diversity-matters. Accessed 14 January 2021.

5. Hann, Christopher. "The Art of Efficiency: How to Do One Thing at a Time." *Entrepreneur*, 1 July 2013, scribd.com/article/327134720/The-Art-Of-Efficiency-How-To-Do-One-Thing-at-A-Time. Accessed 14 January 2021.

6. Jutila, Craig. *Leadership Essentials for Children's Ministry: Passion, Attitude, Teamwork, Honor,* Flagship Church Resources from Group, 2002, pp. 10.

7. Toussaint LL, Owen AD, Cheadle A. "Forgive to live: forgiveness, health, and longevity." *Journal of Behavioral Medicine.* vol. 35, no.4, 2012, pp. 375–86.

HERE'S WHAT PEOPLE HAVE TO SAY ABOUT ESTHER'S NEW BOOK...

Children's ministry requires some serious leadership skills. Children's ministry leaders are connected to babies, preschoolers, elementary kids, students who serve, adults who serve and parents whom they influence. In this role, everything truly does rise and fall on leadership. If you want to be a better leader, Esther lays out a great pathway to guide you and make you a better leader. Check it out and become a better leader.

Dale Hudson
Founder
Building Children's Ministries

"Esther is one the best communicators I have ever met with a contagious passion for children's ministry. This book covers everything you need to know to take your life and ministry to a whole new level. Get your pen and highlighter ready. It's going to be hard to put this one down!"

Ryan Frank
CEO/Publisher
KidzMatter

"A book that will always sit on the top of my desk. Real, extremely practical, encouraging, proven, and insightful, Esther Moreno has written the complete Children's Ministry leadership handbook. This is a must read for kid ministry beginners and veterans. I especially appreciate the Tech Hack, Key Insights, and Discussion Questions that wrap up each chapter. Everything about this book is so so right."

Steve Pennington
Founder
Faithkidz Ministries

"This book is a must have for Children's Ministry Leaders, young and old. This book is PACKED with timeless and yet practical wisdom to not just survive but truly THRIVE in ministry. Esther covers it all. You need this book and the golden nuggets in your life."

Josh Denhart
Founder
KidMinScience.com + LeadMinistry.com

Forget what you think it means to be a progressive leader! Esther Moreno blows that definition out of the water with her new book! Packed full of practical advice, probing questions, and bit-sized leadership nuggets, this book is going to become a "must read" for any Kidmin Leader determined to grow and be effective in a rapidly changing world. Esther has an infectious personality that comes through in her writing! I highly recommend you purchase this book and walk through it with your entire leadership team!

Brian Dollar
Founder of High Voltage Kids Ministry
Author of "I Blew It!" and "Talk Now And Later"

MEET ESTHER MORENO

Esther Moreno is no stranger to ministry. As a daughter of a retired minister, she learned the ins and outs of ministry at an early age. She grew up loving Children's Ministry and patiently awaited the time when she would be old enough to serve as a leader herself. Her absolute favorite thing about growing up in the church was helping her mother create amazing events for the children. She learned then that it doesn't take a big budget to touch the hearts of children, but rather a big heart and an even bigger imagination.

After Esther received her own call into the ministry, she enrolled into Ashland Theological Seminary where she obtained a Master's degree with a concentration in Christian Education. Upon graduation it was no question in her heart as to what she would do next. Within a year's time, Esther had obtained her first ministry position as a Children's Pastor and has been dedicated to that area of ministry ever since.

With over 20 years of Children's Ministry experience, Esther stands by her belief that children are a precious gift from God destined to be cultivated by His design. She believes it is vital that the church not disregard children as lesser members of the body, but rises up to effectively reach these amazing bite-sized contributors to the kingdom of God. Esther is defined by her enthusiasm and energy. She is often met with the question, *"Do you ever get tired?"* to which she responds, *"of Children's Ministry?...No Way!"*

Made in the USA
Monee, IL
16 February 2021

60575822R00090